Spiritual Friendship after Religion

Walking with People while the Rules Are Changing

Joseph A. Stewart-Sicking

 Morehouse Publishing
NEW YORK

For Megan, Sam, and Simon

Morehouse Publishing, 19 East 34th Street, New York, NY 10016

Morehouse Publishing is an imprint of Church Publishing Incorporated.

www.churchpublishing.org

Cover design by Jennifer Kopec, 2Pug Design

Typeset by Denise Hoff

Library of Congress Cataloging-in-Publication Data
Names: Stewart-Sicking, Joseph A., author.
Title: Spiritual friendship after religion : walking with people while the rules are changing / Joseph A. Stewart-Sicking.
Description: New York : Morehouse Publishing, 2016. |
Includes bibliographical references.
Identifiers: LCCN 2015041252 (print) | LCCN 2015041640 (ebook) |
ISBN 9780819232496 (pbk.) | ISBN 9780819232502 (ebook)
Subjects: LCSH: Witness bearing (Christianity) | Friendship—Religious aspects—Christianity.
Classification: LCC BV4520 .S6746 2016 (print) |
LCC BV4520 (ebook) | DDC
248/.5—dc23
LC record available at http://lccn.loc.gov/2015041252

Contents

Foreword

THIS IS A RARE SORT of book, one that combines theory and practice into an inspirational exploration for one's own growth as a spiritual learner and guide. Drawing from a familiar experience of an interfaith coffeehouse conversation with a friend, Joseph Stewart-Sicking leads readers into a surprisingly rich understanding of postmodern culture and faith. Never condemning and never extolling, rather embracing what he calls "critical appreciation" of our times, he explains what shapes the world we inhabit and wonders what—if anything—Christian theology has to do with "fluidity, commodification, control, and diversity," the primary traits of life now.

For those concerned with the future of the church in such challenging circumstances, he suggests one of the greatest gifts of the Christian tradition to the postmodern search for meaning may be the ancient practice of spiritual companionship. With capable hands, he recasts spiritual direction into a generous, inclusive relationship of purposeful friendship, open to a broad range of practitioners and of mutual benefit to both the companion and the one being accompanied along a path toward grace and God. Friendship, not membership in a religious organization or denomination, is the key to transformation, meaning, and the ethical life.

Using four spiritual concerns—change, suffering, joy, and service—as touchstones for exploration, Stewart-Sicking draws wisdom from psychology, theology, and mystical traditions to address the longing for mature character. Throughout, he opens new language to frame our spiritual stories, teaching the practice of theological reflection as a natural and normal part of growth in faith. He urges readers to give up maps in favor of surprise, to surrender to the pleasure of spiritual improvisation. In the process, he models the very relationship he is describing by befriending his readers and encouraging us all onward, offering a kind of teacherly companionship to those who would spend time with his words. The result is both smart and devotional—opening new understanding of the world and new awareness of the God's unexpected presence of love in our lives.

The four frames of postmodern culture and the four frames of spiritual meaning could be pursued in a one-on-one setting between personal friends, in a pastoral counseling setting, between a spiritual director and directee, or in the context of congregation seeking to make their life together more intentional. *Spiritual Friendship after Religion* is less of a directive "how to" book and more of a practical "what if" one. What if we treated all our friendships as the opportunity for the Spirit to show up? What if we encouraged people in our congregations to consider their communal vocation as spiritual companions? What if people of faith took on the task of befriending the postmodern world?

What if this sort of friendship spread? What if?

Diana Butler Bass
Author of *Grounded: Finding God in the World—*
A Spiritual Revolution
Alexandria, Virginia

Preface

THE IDEAS EXPLORED IN THIS book ultimately come back to being a bewildered teacher. As a faculty member in a department of pastoral counseling and spiritual care, I regularly teach classes across our programs, preparing people for pastoral ministry as chaplains and caregivers, training mental-health counselors who integrate spirituality into their practice, and mentoring new scholars exploring the intersection of psychology and the sacred. Because our programs are interfaith and students come from very diverse backgrounds, I am constantly stretched to consider spiritual companioning in new ways.

I have seen many students contemplating ministry in more traditional religious settings struggle, wondering what relevance their training and traditions have in a world where religious categories are rapidly changing. At the same time,

I have seen future therapists wanting to explore the appropriate way to promote spiritual growth through counseling, especially when they do not share a tradition with their clients. Finally, I have directed some intriguing dissertations about how people in our contemporary setting piece together their spirituality, whether in re-creating rites of passage or coming to a deep faith that fits in that middle ground between theism and nontheism. The common question in all of these contexts has been, "What happens to spiritual companionship after established religion?" My own experiences as spiritual director and priest reinforced this question. And as the professor, I had to come up with lectures and reading lists that might give some insight into what is happening.

I have spent a lot of time over the past decade reading the scholarly literature on these phenomena, and I know there are many interesting resources to engage from theology, religious studies, sociology, and psychology. The problem is that relatively few of these would be appropriate to the wide range of students I teach—and this is a problem, since many of these students will be on the front lines of the practice of spiritual companionship as it evolves. There are penetrating philosophical studies of modernity, but these would not suit the master's level students, not only because they are very technical, but also because their description of practice is rarefied and idealized. There are scholarly and popular theological writings, but these tend to assume a Christian perspective, and then, often one that appeals only to a subgroup like mainline protestants, Roman Catholics, evangelicals, or Pentecostals. There are social scientific studies, but these are rarely in conversation with the humanities perspective. Finally, there are classic, modern works on spiritual direction, but few of these give sustained attention to the social changes that are occurring or utilize emerging scholarship.

Thus, I came to this project with the central goal of writing a book that considers the breadth of current scholarship in ways that would be useful to students in all three of the programs I teach in. Having a practical goal in mind has helped me greatly when writing. I give thanks for students in my classes these past two years for challenging my thinking with concrete experiences and stretching me to consider the diversity of relationships that can come under the rubric of spiritual companionship. Any benefit that others get from my writing is largely due to them.

I also have been blessed with an outstanding mentor in Diana Butler Bass, who has been a colleague and dear friend since I first worked with her some fifteen years ago at Christ Church in Alexandria, Virginia. Her deep insights into what is emerging in contemporary spirituality are under the surface of my work here in ways that I cannot even guess. Not only is she a gifted scholar, but she is a gifted writer—two qualities that rarely come together. Better than anyone else I have encountered, Diana can explain the nuances of postmodern social theory and research through such transparent and engaging prose that she has made cutting-edge scholarship accessible to a wide audience without sacrificing its insights. Her advice to me not to be afraid of writing accessibly on complex topics gave me direction at a crucial point in this project.

I also have been blessed through working with Alexander Shaia, whose Quadratos framework for approaching the spiritual life provided an invaluable tool for organizing my thinking on how spirituality is changing. This book is much clearer as a result, and it links the social with the personal in deeper ways.

I want to extend special thanks to colleagues and students at Loyola who have helped this project mature, especially my colleagues Jesse Fox, Tom Rodgerson, Jill Snodgrass, and Bob Wicks; and former PhD students Tucker Brown and Paul Deal. I am looking forward to many more interesting conversations in our future. Thanks are also due to Loyola University Maryland, which provided a sabbatical for the writing of this book.

My editor at Morehouse, Richard Bass, who also is a longtime friend, has sharpened my focus through conversation and feedback, and provided much needed encouragement at key moments in this project. It has been a blessing to entrust my project to him and to benefit from his truly wide range of knowledge and insights.

Finally, I would like to thank my family, especially my mother, Angela Anno, who has given me deep spiritual roots and modeled what ministry should look like in her work as a pastoral counselor.

I am dedicating this book to my wife, Megan, and my sons, Sam and Simon. As a priest herself, Megan has taught me a lot about leadership and good preaching, and her ministry with Immanuel Church in Glencoe, Maryland, has provided many insights about what church can be. Sam and Simon have enriched me—and stretched me—as only children can, and their unique spirits give me a taste of joy.

One final note: Authors are both enriched and bounded by their own locations, and I don't think that any book on spirituality can be otherwise. Therefore, while I try to bring diverse perspectives to my analysis, I cannot avoid writing out of the spiritual traditions that nurture me. I am an Episcopal priest of high-church leanings teaching at a Jesuit institution. My own spiritual formation has come extensively through The Episcopal Church and the Jesuits, with whom I have been associated for over twenty years. I also have been enriched greatly by Tibetan Buddhism at key points of challenge in my life. It is through the lenses of these traditions that I will write, and my hope is that those of other traditions will find insights through, and not despite, them.

CHAPTER I

Just How It Is

I AM A PRIEST WHO is also a professor and a therapist. One of the blessings of this ministry is that I have regular opportunities to talk with people, in a variety of settings, as they negotiate their spiritual lives. Many of these conversations have been where you might expect them: with parishioners whose parents are critically ill, with clients looking to overcome addiction, with students trying to figure out what their studies have to do with their life calling. But surprisingly many—and probably the more interesting ones—have materialized out of conversations that started with a very different purpose with people who have little connection to my "flocks." The following is a great example.

I was sitting in a coffeehouse in Frederick, Maryland, with a friend from high school, one of those good friends with whom it is always easy to pick up even though we have lived in different parts of the country for the past twenty years. We are both professors, so we usually talk about teaching and the politics of higher education. He is a natural scientist and skeptic, and we had an unspoken détente in which we avoided talk about religion. This time was no different. We shared stories of crazy students, talked about life after tenure, then turned to our family lives.

We both had been through some difficult times of grieving recently, and my friend was sharing how he had taken up meditation at the recommendation of a counselor. It had given him a lot of relief, and he shared with me that he was contemplating learning more about Buddhism, but wasn't sure what that was going to entail. He knew I had background in religion, and he wanted my opinion. He was Roman Catholic by upbringing, agnostic through training as a scientist, and usually just indifferent to spirituality or religion. It wasn't part of the furniture of his life. Yet here he was, sitting in a coffeehouse, talking to a friend whom he rarely sees about his fascination with Buddhism. He liked that it was nontheist and empirical, but he was also intrigued by the artwork and ritual of Tibetan Buddhism.

I wasn't sure what to say, so I defaulted to empathic listening as he started to work out what this curiosity meant for him. At the end of our conversation, I mentioned a couple of books on Buddhist spirituality I had found helpful and gently suggested that he might look for a meditation group on his campus. Ninety minutes had passed, and we both returned home and continued our friendship as usual through Facebook and Twitter but did not have another deep discussion until a year later when I visited him. He had enjoyed the books and was now including meditation alongside his regular yoga group. I didn't know whether to count that as a success of spiritual friendship or not.

I doubt that I am alone in finding myself having this kind of conversation more frequently. My experience suggests that there are plentiful opportunities for talking with people about the spiritual life, but frequently, these conversations do not fit the traditional format of spiritual companioning. My friend and I had closeness and frequent digital contact, but only occasional personal contact. He had some familiarity with Christianity, but only a basic level of formation in his Catholic tradition from childhood. He was not sure that spirituality even was a real thing, and his scientific outlook ruled out many traditional expressions of faith as superstition. And yet he also had a very strong social ethic and took part in groups of practice for yoga and sustainable agriculture. His pathway toward spirituality came through the psychotherapeutic use of an Eastern practice, and this practice intrigued him beyond its therapeutic value.

These kinds of conversations—which happen both outside and within organized religious groups—do not meet the assumptions that are behind the classical models of spiritual direction, such as geographical stability, a shared vocabulary for the transcendent, plentiful mentoring opportunities, or lifetime affiliation with a single faith tradition. The primary concern of this book is to explore how the ministry of spiritual companionship can accept the invitation to change posed by this contemporary context.

One blessing for disoriented spiritual companions is that a great deal of social-science research is being conducted on exactly how spirituality and religion are changing. However, the breadth and complexity of this literature require some maps. Observers of contemporary religion and spirituality have pointed to many changes that impact the development of the spiritual life. Consider the following examples:

- Mobility, technology, and globalization have changed the nature of interpersonal relationships.

- Traditional religious organizations and authorities have declined as there has been a proliferation of new and alternate spiritualities.

- The fastest growing group in the United States is the spiritual and religious "nones," now 22 percent of the population.[1]

---

1. "America's Changing Religious Landscape | Pew Research Center," accessed October 6, 2015, http://www.pewforum.org/2015/05/12/americas-changing-religious-landscape/.

- Spirituality has taken on a do-it-yourself character rather than being handed on from one's cultural heritage.

- Spirituality is often encountered as a resource for psychological and physical health, frequently removed from its tradition of origin.

- Spirituality has increasingly become something commodified, marketed, and consumed.

- There are increased encounters between adherents of different faiths, and individuals are increasingly exploring multiple traditions in their own spiritual practices.

- The relationship between science and religion is often presumed to be antagonistic.

- Social and environmental ills engage the political side of many faiths just as many individuals have become alienated from overly political religious expressions.

The list could continue. In fact, scholars don't even agree on what to call the current period—secular? Postmodern? Late capitalist? Post-secular? Post-postmodern? A new Awakening? This is a complicated and rapidly changing picture. To be able to take things in, we can organize these dynamics by four emerging themes: fluidity, commodification, the secular search for control, and diversity.

Fluidity

The lack of agreement on what to call our current era reveals one of its key characteristics, *fluidity*. We don't know precisely what is going on or where we are going because the central characteristics of contemporary social phenomena are "precisely their fragility, temporariness, vulnerability and inclination to constant change."[2] While still modern, our era is different from earlier forms of modernity in which people were certain that scientific progress would slowly improve the human condition and allow everyone to live a good life. Now, the idea of incremental progress is less attractive, replaced by a faith in the power of infinite revision and liquidation.

We value things not for the confidence or certainty they provide, but for how easily they can be abandoned for something else. We can see this change in the enthusiasm for "disruption" and "creative destruction" in the world of business. And our culture values fluidity not just in capital, but also in ideas, organizations, relationships, and selfhood.

The metaphor of fluidity clarifies why so many of the assumptions of the spiritual life seem to be breaking down. A world in which every idea, relationship, and identity is only "for the time being" does not fit well with how spiritual formation is approached in many church environments.

---

2. Zygmunt Bauman, *Liquid Times: Living in an Age of Uncertainty* (Cambridge: Polity Press, 2007), 28. Bauman uses the term *liquid modernity* to describe our current era.

Instead, many structures that have been taken for granted are melting away, some at alarming rates.

Foremost among these is the idea of established religion. Religious organizations and their leaders may have had a special status and authority, but now they are just one voice among the many to which people turn for spiritual advice. In fact, for a growing portion of the population, religious leaders are not compelling enough to even make this cut. There are plenty of therapists, friends, writers, and the Internet to give most of us an overwhelming choice of advice on how to live our lives. Fluidity undercuts the idea of the imprimatur, the "official" source of information that we should all listen to. Denominations as organizations are irrelevant to the practice of spirituality and religion in liquid modernity. This is not to say that the traditions and habits that they carry are no longer of interest. At one and the same time, people are becoming interested in the wisdom of traditions like early Methodism and becoming indifferent to the structures and policies of organizations like the United Methodist Church.

Spirituality has become *open source:*[3] spiritual resources are seen as something shared, and people draw from across sources to piece together something new that works for them. It is the logic of the free and open Internet: Wisdom is not owned by any organization or hierarchy; it should be shared for the bigger common good, regardless of how costly it

---

3. Brian D. McLaren, *Finding Our Way Again: The Return of the Ancient Practices* (Nashville, TN: Thomas Nelson, 2008), 65.

was to create. Open source movements can create new and powerful products, but they are also bad news for the "legacy" organizations that think they should hold the patents.

Fluidity undercuts the rationale of doing something because it is time-tested and traditional. There is no reason for loyalty to the old ways simply because they are old. By contrast, religion intrinsically involves looking to the past for lessons.[4] What is interesting is that spiritual traditions do not seem to be simply going away as we might expect. In fact, turning toward tradition seems to be associated with congregational vitality.[5] Therefore, fluid spirituality is not necessarily becoming more secular and less interested in the past, but the understanding of tradition has undoubtedly changed. Fluid spirituality has little place for custom, doing something simply to reproduce an existing structure, but it has a lot of opening for tradition when seen as a historically embodied argument about wisdom.[6] Tradition in this sense is not Chesterton's "democracy of the dead";[7] it is about bringing the wisdom of the past alive again in new ways.

Finally, fluidity changes the assumptions of what constitutes community, since no single community is central to a life lived in constant change. People are constantly moving, their relationships with others ebbing and flowing,

---

4. Danièle Hervieu-Léger, *Religion as a Chain of Memory* (New Brunswick, NJ: Rutgers University Press, 2000).

5. Diana Butler Bass, *Christianity after Religion: The End of Church and the Birth of a New Spiritual Awakening* (San Francisco: HarperOne, 2012).

6. Alasdair C. MacIntyre, *After Virtue: A Study in Moral Theory*, 2nd ed. (Notre Dame, IN: University of Notre Dame Press, 1984).

7. G. K. Chesterton, *Orthodoxy* (New York: Image Books, 2014), 45.

never keeping shape for long. Throughout each day, people move between several groups: congregation, PTA, yoga group, running group, workplace. Whereas many of these groups would once have been dictated by social convention, most of them now are entered into by choice and based on affinity. People are not living life on their own. The Internet has made it easier than ever for people to find others who share a bewildering array of interests, and contrary to the critique that they are all about dabbling, many of these groups are dedicated to serious practice.[8] But since these groups are chosen, they are unlikely to bring people into encounters with people very different from them. Instead, they provide the security of an "imagined community."[9] And because the focus of these groups is specialized, they often do not last long.

Fluidity creates a unique spiritual situation. It simultaneously opens up new possibilities for leading a meaningful life while depriving us of any standards for judging our success. Spirituality has become "do-it-yourself," and each person's journey can be like that of a nomad: visiting the caravan site from time to time to get new ideas from other travelers, but quickly departing again for the road without any specific destination. The campsite is not especially important beyond being a waypoint, and there is little need for critiquing or investing in it.[10]

---

8. Paul Heelas, *Spiritualities of Life: New Age Romanticism and Consumptive Capitalism* (Malden, MA: Blackwell, 2008).

9. Bauman, *Liquid Times*, 100.

10. Ibid., 23.

Commodification

Fluidity is one face of global capitalism. Another is the unceasing pressure to experience everything in life as a commodity to be obtained and consumed in the most efficient way possible. Consumer spirituality can be shallow and narcissistic, and self-help spirituality has often come in for this kind of criticism.

Any critique that is so easy to make probably hides a lack of nuance. In the case of spirituality as commodity, yes, people do sometimes search for spirituality as if they are finding the best diapers or car or exercise clothing, perhaps with more on the line. As long as there has been religion there have been people looking to buy and sell relics, talismans, shrines, and other spiritual goods. But this kind of sacred economy is more about magic and superstition than spirituality,[11] and magical consumerism has just as much of a history within the walls of the church as outside them. The real dynamics of religious consumerism are much subtler, and we discount many genuine experiences of the divine when we comfort ourselves by making fun of others' spiritual quests.

The relationship between consumerism and spirituality is very complex, but several aspects of it seem especially pertinent to growing in the spiritual life. The first of these is how consumer capitalism creates a way of being in the

---

11. In fact, the sociologist Max Weber goes to great lengths to differentiate magic from religion. There is no church of magic. Max Weber, *The Sociology of Religion* (Boston: Beacon Press, 1963).

Spirituality as Commodity

world (shaping our understanding, experiences, and actions) that defines human life in terms of infinite freedom, unlimited resources, and self-focused choices. Living this way tends to turn religion into a kind of cheap transcendence, Christotainment, or "special effect."[12] When we want to feel "spiritual" (because in this world, spirituality is a kind of peak experience), we listen to chanting monks, sit in a darkened auditorium while a praise band performs, or place icons and mandalas around our room. We become spiritual gluttons, susceptible to our faith's falling apart as soon as we no longer are "feeling it."[13]

Even more insidiously, consuming spirituality as a commodity has the effect of hiding the ways and purposes for which that spiritual item was created. Christianity, which has the potential to turn society upside down, can be reduced to comforting platitudes, as unthreatening and bastardized as the Che Guevara T-shirt sold in the local big box store. And spiritual community, which has the power to transform lives, can become a sort of aspirational brand identity—which necessarily excludes those different from us.

Consumer spirituality also focuses on technology as the model and vehicle of transformation. The message is straightforward: press a button, take this pill, meditate for

---

12. Graham Ward, *The Politics of Discipleship: Becoming Postmaterial Citizens.* (Grand Rapids, MI: Baker Academic, 2009), 148.

13. This is not solely a modern phenomenon. John of the Cross describes this phenomenon in his treatment of the dark night of the senses. Commodification complicates this by making other aspects of faith atrophy.

this length of time, use this program, visit this place, set your mind on God's prosperity . . . and things will work together seamlessly to meet your needs. This "device paradigm" abstracts things from their material settings and makes them disposable, interchangeable, glamorous.[14] You buy the machine. You own it. And don't worry, because there are geniuses producing better and better machines to meet your needs down the line.

When spirituality is experienced as a commodity, then it is inevitably judged by its therapeutic value. There is nothing wrong with faith being therapeutic, generally speaking. Jesus promises complete joy, and Scripture promises comfort amid distress. Many of the characteristic doctrines of the church have developed out of a pastoral sensibility that links faith to the pursuit of happiness.[15] The problem created by consumer spirituality is that its idea of happiness is too thin. The therapeutic can be reduced to the *merely* therapeutic without anyone noticing, and the richness of a way of life can be turned into a utilitarianism that sees faith as something like wheat grass—usually unpleasant, but good for you.[16] And a faith that can be functionally compared to a pill is not

---

14. Albert Borgmann, *Power Failure: Christianity in the Culture of Technology* (Grand Rapids, MI: Brazos Press, 2003), 17.

15. Ellen T. Charry, *By the Renewing of Your Minds: The Pastoral Function of Christian Doctrine* (New York: Oxford University Press, 1997).

16. Here, it matches up with the Moralistic Therapeutic Deism that Smith has observed among teens and young adults in the first decade of the twenty-first century. Christian Smith et al., *Lost in Transition: The Dark Side of Emerging Adulthood* (New York: Oxford University Press, 2011).

threatening in any way to the powers and principalities of this world. Consumption inhibits critical thinking, and there is no room for spiritual ideas such as the Christian practices of giving one's self for others and living simply.

The good news where consumerism and spirituality are concerned is that spirituality contains seeds of resistance that, if nurtured, can rip apart the logic of consumerism from within. Many spiritual practices, such as meditation, hospitality, and singing, have benefits that can be obtained only through the practice itself. Such practices are pursued for their own sake, and they look to a tradition for standards of excellence that can lead us in further training.[17] Research has repeatedly demonstrated the potency of these kinds of practices as people move from dabblers to serious practitioners. Even in the supposedly consumerist and therapeutic spiritual scenes of the yoga session or the growth group, practitioners can begin to get interested in the practices for their own sake, often reproducing the structure of monastic communities (gurus, ongoing practice spaces, traditions, spiritual guidance) while steadfastly insisting that they are not "religious."[18] It is a powerful thing to open oneself

---

17. MacIntyre, *After Virtue*.

18. In *Spiritualities of Life*, Heelas has an extended refutation, grounded in field research, of the claim that these spiritualities are necessarily consumeristic. Courtney Bender also has shown that communities of practice take on structure even among those who eschew the very idea of structure, such as those in New Age movements. See Courtney Bender, *The New Metaphysics: Spirituality and the American Religious Imagination* (Chicago: University of Chicago Press, 2010).

to the depth of the Spirit, and all of us are in over our heads in terms of what we can expect from our spiritual practices. They can lead us to totally reorient our lives and provide us with a passion that we didn't know we could have.

The Secular Search for Control

Understanding the spiritual situation of the West inevitably involves answering the question of how it has moved from "a society in which it was virtually impossible not to believe in God to one in which faith, even for the staunchest believer, is one human possibility among others."[19] Understanding secularism in this sense, as a change in the conditions under which belief happens, is key to understanding the way spirituality now plays out.

The philosopher Charles Taylor has identified two conditions necessary for this form of secularity to have developed.[20] First, the culture must have made a strong distinction between the natural and supernatural, often based on theological principles. Second, as an unintended consequence of this distinction, it came to be seen as possible to live entirely within the natural arena without reference

---

19. Charles Taylor, *A Secular Age* (Cambridge, MA: Belknap Press of Harvard University Press, 2007), 3.

20. Charles Taylor, "Afterword: Apologia pro Libro Suo," in *Varieties of Secularism in a Secular Age*, ed. Michael Warner, Jonathan VanAntwerpen, and Craig Calhoun (Cambridge, MA: Harvard University Press, 2010).

to transcendent reality (if indeed there were such a thing). Taylor calls this perspective the *immanent frame*. Life in the immanent frame disenchants the world, but it has the benefit of buffering the self from contact with supernatural entities. People no longer have to worry about demons or magic or spirits, since these are irrelevant and probably meaningless.

This development is framed as reason's triumph over outdated and superstitious illusions that have limited human progress. Freed of the meaningless gloss of the sacred, people are free to see the reality of human nature and to work to improve it scientifically. Taylor notes that the way in which modernity tells this story is through subtraction: "This is no more than ___"; "What is really happening is ___"; "The real truth about Jesus is that ___"; "I have no need for that hypothesis." We get rid of overly complicated explanations that involve entities beyond our control (such as God) in favor of simpler ones that give us the ability to control things for our own purposes. The result is a flatter, simpler world, but one that seems predictable.

This worldview has an internal tension. Human life requires a global sense of meaning,[21] even if the meaning we live by is that there is no meaning. This in turn requires a sense that there is a fullness/wholeness/depth to reality. The immanent frame is supposed to be able to be inhabited without any reference to anything beyond it. Talk of fullness, whether arising from the natural world or transcending it, goes against the clarity and predictability that the immanent frame is supposed to

---

21. Viktor E. Frankl, *Man's Search for Meaning* (Boston: Beacon Press, 2006).

provide. Therefore, when there are experiences of some fullness breaking through into our reality, these are fragile and subject to argument.[22] With each new epiphany, ways of experiencing fullness multiply, leading to an explosion of new spiritual options as people search for contact with depth.

This analysis highlights a key spiritual challenge. The default, scientific position of modern thought precludes the ability to conceive of reality in ways that were critical to prior generations of spirituality. There is no demonic, but there is no grace as well. There are no "thin places." Science and technology should solve all our problems, and if we still suffer, it is because we are ignorant or not using them well. It is not tragic. Important spiritual concepts, such as the soul, which exists in the trust and invitation of the Other, are lost and inaccessible.[23]

This emphasis on certainty and control is not the only way of living in the world, even if it is a prominent one. There are other modern modes of existence, for example, law, technology, religion, fiction.[24] Each has its own chain of reasoning that flourishes or flounders under specific conditions. As a result, many problems of modernity stem from category mistakes, judging one way of being modern according to the standards of another.

---

22. Taylor, "Afterword: Apologia pro Libro Suo."

23. Rowan Williams, *Lost Icons: Reflections on Cultural Bereavement* (Harrisburg, PA: Morehouse, 2000).

24. Bruno Latour, *An Inquiry into Modes of Existence: An Anthropology of the Moderns* (Cambridge, MA: Harvard University Press, 2013).

Modern science is obsessed with finding the naked, unadulterated, and indisputable facts of the world and transmitting them to others without any mediation, bias, or alteration.[25] It is in search of "nothing but the facts," assuming those can be known. The dominance of this framework, known as positivism, leads to its being imposed on religion, with the result that religion and spirituality tend to accept the terms of debate from the positivist worldview. This leaves spirituality and religion with the choice between translating itself into secular terms or into an antirational fundamentalism. It comes to believe in "belief."[26] The very speech that once motivated people to change the world becomes unspeakable, a bunch of meaningless terms from a metaphysical debate in another century.

In the fundamentalist/modernist framework, religion loses its soul. Religious speech transforms and converts those who receive it. It is not detached or objective.[27] Its unfathomable depth leads it through an endless cycle of affirmation and denial, constantly renewing itself while seeking to be faithful to its origins, confounding those who want to contain its meaning. God is not a thing to be grasped. This makes talk of the Spirit fundamentally opposed to positivism, and it means

---

25. Latour refers to this mode of existence as "double click," evoking the way in which hyperlinks seem to magically make pure information appear immediately, without any account of how it got there.

26. Latour, *An Inquiry*, 313.

27. Latour, *An Inquiry*.

that spirituality has to always answer the charge that it is meaningless in a time in which positivism is in the driver's seat.

Diversity

A final theme emerging from recent scholarship is spiritual diversity, seen clearly in recent demographic studies.[28] Immigration and access to information have increased the number of religious/spiritual traditions to which people are exposed. Buddhists, Muslims, and Hindus each comprise 1 percent of the US population, and these proportions are growing. Twenty-four percent of married Americans report that their spouse is of a different religious tradition. An equal number report belief in reincarnation, the power of crystals, and astrology. Twenty-two percent of Americans are religiously unaffiliated, forming the plurality in twenty-three states. In short, people have many more choices and less belief that theirs is the only way, and they often combine multiple traditions in ways that traditional spiritual direction did not anticipate.

Christianity was born in an era of great religious diversity, but contemporary pluralism has its own characteristic set of challenges. As faiths come into contact with one another in

---

28. Public Religion Research Institute, "PRRI—American Values Atlas," accessed October 6, 2015, http://ava.publicreligion.org/; "Religious Landscape Study," *Pew Research Center's Religion & Public Life Project*, accessed October 6, 2015, http://www.pewforum.org/religious-landscape-study/.

the modern world, they must navigate issues such as dialogue and relationships among groups, conversion and proselytizing, relations between majority and minority groups, multiple belonging, cooperation among groups, faith in the public square, peacebuilding, and fundamentalisms.[29] Added to the complexity is the fact that the other aspects of modernity interact with this dynamic.

Diversity calls for a response, and the theologian Paul Knitter provides a helpful summary of these responses: "only one true religion," "the one fulfills the many," "many true religions called to dialogue," and "many religions: so be it."[30] This is not just an exercise for scholars. Each individual has to find ways to understand diversity and choose among these options. Our answers shape our spiritual lives in profound ways. If we think our tradition is the one and only true one or that other religions are fulfilled in it, our interest in learning from those of different faiths decreases. At the very least, we will find it difficult to work with these other groups on shared projects. We will also miss opportunities for growth in our own faith through dealing with difference. More pluralist approaches, such as dialogue and acceptance, can enrich our spiritual lives through encounters with the other, but they

---

29. David Cheetham, Douglas Pratt, and David Thomas, "Introduction," in *Understanding Interreligious Relations*, ed. David Cheetham, Douglas Pratt, and David Thomas (Oxford: Oxford University Press, 2013).

30. Paul F. Knitter, *Introducing Theologies of Religions* (Maryknoll, NY: Orbis Books, 2002).

bring the risk of staying on the surface of our own and others' traditions to create a false spirit of hospitality.

In addition, diversity is not just a reality between faith groups. While we remember that there are different denominations within each religion, we tend to treat each denomination as monolithic. Some of the most challenging diversity to handle in the spiritual life is disagreement with people in our own faith communities who seem authentic in their faith but differ with us in belief or practice. These encounters call some of our basic assumptions into question, and we can't just dismiss them as other or mistaken since they appear to have come to their approach through the same traditions as we have.

Some recent theology can exacerbate this tendency to homogenize our faith communities. In response to modernist approaches that see religion as being about certain fundamental truths or as the attempt to put a special kind of experience into words, theologians in the postliberal approach have favored seeing religion as a cultural and linguistic reality, a way of life comprised of practices rooted in a tradition.[31]

There are many benefits to this approach, such as stressing the distinctiveness of faith as a way of life and not just beliefs or experiences. However, the shorthand version of this theology tends to talk about engaging "*the* tradition," as if traditions were well defined and well regulated. The

---

31. The foundational text of this movement is George A. Lindbeck, *The Nature of Doctrine: Religion and Theology in a Postliberal Age* (Philadelphia: Westminster Press, 1984).

reality is that traditions are more of a style than a set of identical items.[32] No one polices the boundaries of traditions, even if there is consensus on their core ideas. In this way, contemporary diversity changes the very content of traditions as people come into contact with different denominations and religions and their ideas diffuse into one another.

In upcoming chapters, we will examine these four trends as they impact different parts of the spiritual life. But first, we must make a choice: How should we understand these phenomena? For each of them, there is a vocal contingent of commentators who see their job purely as one of critique— to the extent that contemporary spirituality diverges from classical norms, it needs to be confronted and reshaped. There are also cheerleaders for adapting to these new trends, accepting their internal logic as unambiguously good for religious traditions. I think the wisest approach is in between, a critical appreciation. None of these is entirely good or bad; they just are how it is. They are the setting, and they can be transformed by grace. Some trends create specific challenges for spiritual formation as traditionally understood. Other trends indicate that the serious cultivation of spirituality tends to be a resilient phenomenon and that there are new manifestations of spiritual friendship that can be drawn upon in moving forward.

---

32. Kathryn Tanner, *Theories of Culture: A New Agenda for Theology* (Minneapolis: Fortress Press, 1997).

In taking this approach, I differ from some authors[33] in assuming that there is much to be learned from contemporary spiritual trends outside the bounds of the Church and that the spiritual lives of those who practice them are not necessarily lacking when compared to those of many churchgoers. The Czech priest and psychologist Tomáš Halík provides a helpful illustration from the experience of the Church after the Velvet Revolution:

> When . . . Christ's followers came out freely into the open after so many years, they noticed many people who applauded them and maybe a few who had previously shaken their fists at them. What they didn't notice, however, was that the trees all around them were full of Zacchaeuses—those who were unwilling or unable to join the throng of old or brand-new believers, but were neither indifferent nor hostile to them. Those Zacchaeuses were curious seekers, but at the same time they wanted to maintain a certain distance. That odd combination of inquisitiveness and expectation, interest and shyness, and sometimes, maybe, even a feeling of guilt and

---

33. See for example Lillian Daniel, *When Spiritual but Not Religious Is Not Enough: Seeing God in Surprising Places, Even the Church* (London: Hodder & Stoughton, 2013).

"inadequacy," kept them hidden in their fig trees.[34]

A similar challenge now faces religion in the Western world: as church attendance drops, we tend to notice those loud voices of secularization and those bright spots within our existing religious structures. But Jesus suggests that we notice the Zacchaeuses, those who would be interested in engaging us if we just learned to speak their names. Zacchaeuses are not limited to the "nones" or the "spiritual but not religious." The same trends that create that mixture of interest and shyness about faith outside of the church are operating in the church, and the borders between "insiders" and "outsiders" are fuzzy. We do not always have recourse to our traditional models of spiritual friendship even within parish ministry. And this can be good.

---

34. Tomáš Halík, *Patience with God: The Story of Zacchaeus Continuing in Us,* Kindle edition (New York: Doubleday, 2009), Kindle locations 166–71.

Questions for Discussion

1 Think about conversations you have had recently with people who might be considered "Zacchaeuses." How did these emerge? What kind of settings, situations, and relationships made them possible? What can make them difficult to recognize?

2 Which of the four contemporary dynamics impacting spirituality (fluidity, commodification, the secular search for control, and diversity) were most familiar? Least familiar? Do you think they are equally important? Why or why not?

3 Is your first impulse to see the dangers or the opportunities in contemporary spiritual trends? What does this suggest is important to you as a spiritual companion? How might you learn from the other tendency without sacrificing the insights that your perspective gives?

For Further Reading

Bass, Diana Butler. *Christianity After Religion: The End of Church and the Birth of a New Spiritual Awakening*. San Francisco: HarperOne, 2012. A survey of contemporary religious trends arguing that these changes constitute a new spiritual awakening.

Bauman, Zygmunt. *Liquid Modernity*. Malden, MA: Blackwell, 2000. An overview of Bauman's account of liquidity.

Heelas, Paul. *Spiritualities of Life*: *New Age Romanticism and Consumptive Capitalism*. Malden, MA: Blackwell, 2008. An in-depth examination of alternative spiritualities moving beyond surface criticisms of their consumer nature.

An Inquiry into Modes of Existence. http://www.modesof existence.org. The online home of Bruno Latour's research into types of modernity. Comprehensive, but requires effort.

The Pluralism Project. http://www.pluralism.org. The online home of the Pluralism Project at Harvard University, which explores the varieties and dynamics of religious pluralism.

Smith, James K. A. *How (Not) to Be Secular: Reading Charles Taylor*. Grand Rapids MI: Eerdmans, 2014. An introduction to Taylor's thought on secularism with a proposal for resisting some of these changes.

CHAPTER 2

Being a Spiritual Companion

LUIDITY, COMMODIFICATION, CONTROL, AND DIVER-
SITY are changing the shape of the spiritual life. But
while our assumptions about what spiritual companionship looks like may need to change, the need for these
relationships is not going away. As we see more Zacchaeuses
and have more interfaith coffee-shop conversations, we are
reminded of how important it is for people to have safe relationships in which they can honestly explore their spiritual
lives. If anything, the need is greater than ever before, since
fewer people take part in organizations that offer this kind
of relationship. For those of us who feel called to be spiritual
companions, this is an opportunity.

The answer to this opportunity is not simply to get people into churches, nor is it to give up our traditional models of spiritual companionship in order to keep up with the times. Neither one will work. For all its benefits, being involved in a congregation does not insulate us from social changes, and it is not a guarantee of honest and safe spiritual relationships. And any deep exploration of the spiritual life will need a relationship with an experienced practitioner that looks like traditional spiritual direction. The times are changing, but accepting change calls for patience and discernment. It is not time to have a plan; it is time to improvise.

For this reason, it is helpful to consider spiritual companionship in its broadest sense, neither ignoring new forms nor giving up on the wisdom of classic ones. Whether coming from a psychotherapist, clergy member, spiritual director, yoga instructor, or old friend, all spiritual companionship is characterized by a special form of friendship that offers a space of freedom in which we can be honestly ourselves and explore our deepest spiritual longings. Regardless of the context, spiritual companionship is based in spiritual friendship.

Spiritual Friendship

The love that characterizes friendship is essential to the spiritual life, even if it seems like dramatic forms of love such as desire and self-sacrifice receive more attention. In the

Christian tradition, one of the most insightful explorations of this love is seen in the *Spiritual Friendship* of Aelred of Rievaulx, an English Cistercian abbot of the twelfth century. Aelred's description of spiritual friendship provides a good guide to what kinds of relationships we should pursue today for mutual spiritual enrichment.

For Aelred, spiritual friendship is the "guardian of the spirit," the love and sweetness that unite people who share the pursuit of the good life.[1] The invitation at the beginning of his discussion gives a vivid picture of this love:

> Here we are, you and I, and I hope that Christ makes a third with us. No one can interrupt us now, no one can spoil our friendly conversation; no one's voice or noise will break in upon this pleasant solitude of ours. So come now, dearest friend, reveal your heart and speak your mind. You have a friendly audience; say whatever you wish. And let us not be ungrateful for this time or for our opportunity and leisure.[2]

In spiritual friendship, we not only encourage each other toward goodness, we share a solitude in which we feel God's

---

1. Aelred of Rievaulx, *Spiritual Friendship*, trans. Mary Eugenia Laker (Kalamazoo, MI: Cistercian Publications, 1974), 55.
2. Aelred, *Spiritual Friendship*, 29.

presence as we reveal our deepest thoughts and desires. This description is similar to the Celtic tradition of the *anam ċara*, or soul friend, "someone to whom you confessed, revealing the hidden intimacies of your life. With the anam ċara you could share your inner-most self, your mind and your heart. This friendship was an act of recognition and belonging. When you had an anam ċara, your friendship cut across all convention, morality, and category."[3] This kind of spiritual friendship is still something that cuts against convention, but it is possible to have, even amid all of our culture's dynamics that push us toward brief and shallow engagement. And wherever we find it, we should nourish it.

Aelred describes four qualities that are essential for spiritual friendship: loyalty, right intention for the relationship, discretion, and patience. Are these possible in today's culture? On the surface, we can easily name trends that would make them difficult.

Fluidity brings us into and out of people's lives and always has us looking for something better. Obviously this makes loyalty difficult and can distract us from being intentional or having patience.

A focus on commodified happiness can distract us from the benefits of long-term friendship that take patience to develop.

---

3. John O'Donohue, *Anam Ċara: A Book of Celtic Wisdom* (New York: Cliff Street Books, 1997), 13–14.

Technology can both bring us more contact with others and make that contact less personal.

Diversity means that it takes work to understand someone on a personal level.

Friendship faces many challenges in our society, and the decline in community and in the breadth of social relationships is well documented in research.[4] But it seems to me that friendship is such a fundamental human need that we will always find ways to resist its disappearance. And the reality is that even despite these challenges, many of us still are blessed with the kind of friendships that can nourish our spiritual lives. It is important to make an effort to keep them; they are, actually, pretty resilient, able to be picked up in a coffeehouse after months apart.

Knowledge and Skills

Spiritual friendship is necessary for any relationship to nurture our spiritual lives, but is it sufficient for us to grow? The answer depends on where we find ourselves on the spiritual path. Supportive spiritual friendships can be a source of grace and energy for our spiritual development, but some of the circumstances we face require more specialized knowledge and experience. Spiritual companionship is a continuum of

---

4. Robert D. Putnam, *Bowling Alone: The Collapse and Revival of American Community* (New York: Simon & Schuster, 2001).

relationships, some more formal or focused than others. It is important to know whether more expertise is needed when we confront a spiritual challenge. Otherwise, we might find ourselves in the position of Teresa of Ávila, who tells the story of a bad spiritual director who told her to make a crude gesture to visions sent to her from God (it didn't work out well).[5]

Spiritual companionship has core competencies to master. To borrow from a famous definition, spiritual companioning is a relationship that helps one recognize, experience, and respond to the fullness of being.[6] To do this, spiritual companions must at minimum have knowledge about what spiritual experience and growth looks like in their friends' traditions, as well as knowledge of psychology and human transformation. They also need to have experience in attending to their own spiritual lives so as to be able to recognize the challenges and paths of spiritual growth. Finally, spiritual companions need to be committed to their own spiritual practice and rooted in the wisdom that comes from sustained engagement with at least one tradition.

Many relationships might, therefore, qualify as spiritual companioning. This includes traditional spiritual directors with formal training, but it also might describe the many other figures we encounter along our spiritual

---

5. Teresa of Ávila, "The Book of Her Life," in *The Collected Works of St. Teresa of Ávila,* trans. Kieran Kavanaugh and Otilio Rodriguez, vol. 1 (Washington, DC: Institute of Carmelite Studies, 1976), Ch. 29.5.

6. William A. Barry and William J. Connolly, *The Practice of Spiritual Direction* (1982; New York: HarperOne, 2009), 8.

quest: therapists, clergy, leaders and members of a group devoted to practice, fellow parishioners, personal friends. The personal characteristics Aelred describes need to be present for any such relationship to nourish us. In addition, we need a companion who is capable of helping us recognize, experience, and respond to the fullness of being. Therefore, the important consideration is whether the potential companion has experience and wisdom dealing with the aspects of the spiritual life and the experiences we are facing.

For what this might look like outside of formal spiritual direction, we might look to the lay-focused and group-driven Wesleyan class system, in which much of the spiritual companioning takes places through covenanted groups of peers, but those with specific issues of spiritual growth are paired with one or more others who are experienced in this area.[7] There is also the indirect supervision of pastors to provide appropriate guidance. This system could be realized in many contexts in contemporary society, not just congregations. I wonder whether some of the most enriching spiritual conversations going on right now might be in brewing clubs or mom's groups.

It is important to remember that spiritual formation happens through the entirety of our lives; we should capitalize on those relationships that provide positive formation wherever

7. Wesley Tracy, "Spiritual Direction in the Wesleyan-Holiness Tradition," in *Spiritual Direction and the Care of Souls: A Guide to Christian Approaches and Practices*, ed. Gary W. Moon and David G. Benner (Downers Grove, IL: InterVarsity Press, 2004).

we find them. The important thing is to discern whether the formation we are giving and receiving is good. When we and our spirits are livened through our relationships to become who we are called to be, even to do things that we know will be difficult, that is often a sign of good formation. When our relationships puff us up with spiritual candy, discourage us, or let us off the hook, we might want to look elsewhere.[8] Finally, when spiritual companions find themselves dealing with matters beyond their expertise, they need to send their friends to trustworthy professionals who will be more appropriate.

Movements of the Spiritual Life

While spiritual guidance in the Christian tradition has many models for growth and change in the spiritual life (the most common being the triple way of purgation, illumination, and union), these derive from monastic models that assume a degree of stability not always present, especially for those in our society who are only beginning to contemplate deepening their spiritual lives. A useful alternative, from the work of the neo-Jungian Alexander Shaia, identifies a recurring cycle of four spiritual tasks, referred to as Quadratos.[9]

---

8. This is a condensed form of Ignatius Loyola's rules for discernment, which is itself a much more complex practice that can be explored more formally. See Ignatius Loyola, *The Spiritual Exercises of St. Ignatius*, trans. Anthony Mottola (Garden City, NY: Image Books, 1964).

9. Alexander J. Shaia with Michelle Gaugy, *The Hidden Power of the Gospels: Four Questions, Four Paths, One Journey* (San Francisco: HarperOne, 2010).

Shaia's model emerged from his reflection on how the Church has gone about presenting the four distinct Gospel accounts of Jesus. As liturgy developed, there emerged the three-year lectionary cycle of Scripture readings for worship that presented the Gospels in a particular order: Matthew, Mark, then Luke, with John's Gospel primarily encountered each year at Lent and Eastertide. Shaia posits that this order is meant to be formative and that the perspectives of each Gospel's depiction of Jesus follow a great map of transformation centered around four questions: How do we face change (Matthew)? How do we move through suffering (Mark)? How do we receive joy (John)? and How do we mature in service (Luke)? Drawing on Jungian insights, Shaia points out the recurrence of this pattern in artwork, story, and the seasons, suggesting that it is an archetypal pattern of four moments in the spiritual life.

This model is applicable across a wide range of circumstances and gets at the fundamental features of spirituality. It also gives explicit attention to change and service, which tend to be downplayed in the focus on developing prayer that characterizes the typologies of traditional ascetical theology. In the following chapters we will explore each of these movements in light of current cultural dynamics and suggest how spiritual friendship can respond.

Questions for Discussion

1 The chapter argues that many relationships outside the church (e.g., psychotherapists) can be valuable for spiritual friendship. Can you identify any of these relationships in your own life? How is their potential to be spiritually transforming affected by their lack of an ecclesial setting?

2 At what point, if any, in the spiritual life is formal spiritual direction necessary? Why?

3 Of Aelred's characteristics of a spiritual friendship (loyalty, right intention for the relationship, discretion, and patience), which are easiest and which are hardest to achieve in your setting? What concrete steps could you take to foster them?

For Further Reading

Chapman, John. *Spiritual Letters.* London: Burns & Oates, 2003. Insightful examples of spiritual friendship from a modern Benedictine author.

Francis de Sales and Jeanne-Françoise de Chantal, *Francis de Sales, Jane de Chantal: Letters of Spiritual Direction.* Classics of Western Spirituality. Translated by Wendy M. Wright and Joseph F. Power. New York: Paulist Press, 1988. Moving examples of spiritual friendship from two seventeenth century authors and friends.

Guenther, Margaret. *Holy Listening: The Art of Spiritual Direction.* Cambridge, MA: Cowley Publications, 1992. An introduction to spiritual companioning.

CHAPTER 3

Change as a Spiritual Issue

T O UNDERSTAND THE SPIRITUAL LIFE, you have to understand change. Our contemporary society should make this clear, but it is not often seen as a basic spiritual task. We tend to focus on morality, salvation, or experience as the basic spiritual areas. But as beings embedded in time, change surrounds us, even if we are oblivious to it. Buddhist spirituality provides a penetrating analysis of this reality through the concept of *dukkha*, the unavoidable and painful unsatisfactoriness of life.

We suffer through the changes brought by aging and disease, through hanging on to momentary comforts, and through the very transitory nature of every pleasant thing. Every once in a while, we awaken to this pain of change. But dealing with change is a spiritual opportunity as well—change makes conversion and growth possible. Change means that the images and idols we substitute for God will inevitably prove unworthy of our faith. Ultimately, change is an invitation we can accept or ignore.

Shaia identifies dealing with change as the first path of the spiritual life and draws out several aspects of its progression. Initially, the invitation to embrace change appears through discomfort or estrangement, a sense that "the small self we have been, spiritually and psychologically, is just not up to dealing with the life we live."[1] But it takes time to be receptive to this invitation. Very often, we are not willing to hear this message. Yet eventually, we are overwhelmed and we realize that "there is no place that does not see you. You must change your life."[2] And we consent to move forward.

Things are not effortless or straightforward. Accepting the invitation to change involves dying to self and saying yes again and again as we become distracted by our worldly concerns and discouraged by our missteps. The role of the spiritual companion in the face of change is to highlight the tensions present, to confront the delusion that things can remain as they are, and to provide stability and support so that one's friend can say yes again and again to God's invitation.

---

1. Shaia, *Hidden Power*, 43.

2. Rainer Maria Rilke, "Archaic Torso of Apollo," in *Ahead of All Parting: The Selected Poetry and Prose of Rainer Maria Rilke*, trans. Stephen Mitchell (New York: Modern Library, 1995).

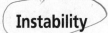 Instability

The fluid nature of contemporary society both helps and hinders the process of engaging change. The structures that might provide a stable environment for exploring change are melting away, chief among them the program-oriented congregation that is often assumed to be there for those serious about the spiritual life. And yet, the demise of their current forms confronts us with the necessity of dealing with change. Fluidity asks us to consider the practice of stability in new ways.

Precisely as they experimented with fleeing the world, the monastic traditions of Christianity discovered how fundamental stability is to spiritual maturity. Confronted on every side by demons and temptation, the desert dwellers learned through experience that they needed to rely on the wisdom of elders in order to merely endure, let alone thrive. In leaving the old social order behind, they found that even a hermit needs to be anchored in order not to become spiritually adrift.

The wisdom that came from this experience was codified in the Rule of St. Benedict, which includes a vow of stability,[3] in which the monk promises commitment to a particular community, to "bloom where you're planted." Fluid modernity, with its transitory, negotiated relationships, is directly opposed

---

3. Benedict, *The Rule of St. Benedict in English*, trans. Timothy Fry (New York: Vintage Books, 1998), 58.

to pursuing this vow, and in this way, it is directly opposed to the foundation one needs for spiritual maturity and dealing with change. Fluidity provides endless change, but never allows us to see that change as an invitation to growth.

One clear example of this pattern is the way in which relationships tend to be episodic and shallow. While we have shared spaces that may be "public," they are not "civil."[4] People do not tend to engage one another, even if they are in the same place. We tend to ignore the good and bad examples of others, which gives us few models for how to live. A key part of the wisdom of stability is that growth rarely happens without friction. As a Franciscan student of mine once put it, "knowing that you are stuck in community with all these people who irritate you in unique ways" is a tremendous spiritual challenge. You must change your life to live in community. Fluid relationships let people be alone together, getting what they want without worrying about how that impacts others.

The response of spiritual leaders to these challenges is often to conserve the structures that have served us in the past. Several authors have noted the unique benefits of the parish, a place where there are the kind of ongoing and challenging interactions that allow members to shape one another's lives.[5] But they often have done so in order

---

4. Baumann, *Liquid Modernity*.

5. Daniel, *When Spiritual but Not Religious Is Not Enough*; Andrew Davison and Alison Milbank, *For the Parish: A Critique of Fresh Expressions* (London: SCM Press, 2010).

to critique the seriousness of those who attempt to cultivate spirituality outside of these structures. The problem is that perfection in Christian community was not achieved in the 1950s, the 1200s, the 300s, or even in the Apostolic Age. It is also not being achieved through new forms of church today. Fluidity may be a challenge, but it forces spiritual leaders to keep from being too attached to any one manifestation of being spiritual together.

Faith Shopping

While fluidity both demands and challenges our ability to accept change, our culture of commodities attempts to distract us from it. Capitalism manufactures an endless parade of things to desire, one after the other. It creates dissatisfaction that could lead to meaningful change only to short-circuit this process by offering a quick and easy way to fulfill our desires. The kind of change it wants is really no change at all—in switching brands or trying a new product we will still be the same potential consumers who can be sold the next big thing. We are never allowed to consider that our current way of living is not up to the deepest calls on our lives. Really confronting change requires us to be uncomfortable, and the promise of consumer capitalism is that we never need to be uncomfortable for long.

Teresa of Ávila gave an evocative description of this process in her discussion of the beginning stages of the spiritual life in the Interior Castle.[6] She says that the only way to enter into the spiritual life is through self-knowledge, but that even as we try to become more intimate with God, countless concerns about our social status, business, and lifestyle come with us into our soul like so many reptiles and vermin, distracting us from getting to know our true selves. It takes effort and help to keep our focus on what is truly important. Teresa points out what a shame it is that people have God dwelling in their innermost selves and yet they don't give any thought to this intimate connection when going about their lives.

If wellness is a commodity to be purchased, it ultimately puts the power and blame for our happiness in our own hands. If we are overcome with ennui, it is because we haven't found the right solution yet and implemented it. We don't lack patience; we lack resources. Unfortunately, accepting the invitation to change inevitably involves admitting that we are powerless to make our lives into the lives we know God is calling us to. True change requires us to rely on grace, and you can't sell anything to God, so a culture of commodification tries to convince us that change is easier than it is, just a click away.

---

6. Teresa of Ávila, "The Interior Castle," in *The Collected Works of St. Teresa of Avila*, trans. Kieran Kavanaugh and Otilio Rodriguez, vol. 2 (Washington, DC: Institute of Carmelite Studies, 1976).

Searching for Depth in a Flat World

The fascination of modern culture with control has led to the loss of some images for the spiritual life that have real effects on how we approach change. Modernity tends to see the world as a bunch of stuff without its own purposes, waiting for us to find scientific ways to use it efficiently for whatever we would like. The idea of the soul, something we patiently cultivate through relationships with that which is greater than us, is lost. And we also lose the ability to identify spiritual change when it can't be modeled as a machine or pill. The result is that we can't recognize spiritual change for what it is.

I often think of the experience I had with the garden at a new rectory. I wanted to be conscientious about keeping the garden in good shape, so when I saw some odd red stems sprouting in an area where I thought we were supposed to have tulips, I resolved to pull them up. Busy as I was, I never got around to it—which was a good thing, since they turned out to be large peony bushes with some of the most beautiful flowers in the whole garden. Dealing with change requires the patience to allow new and fragile shoots to mature, as we often don't recognize what is growing or how it will mature.

By flattening away the spiritual dimension, the modern emphasis on control has eliminated the ability to see new spiritual life. And if we can't see these stirrings of the spirit, we are likely to neglect or uproot them. The basic metaphors of modern science are closer to programming than gardening—we assume away those parts of the problem that are not under our control. Talk of depth or mystery tends to be seen as woo-woo hand-waving, something that appeals to simpletons or inveterate mystics. But the question of spiritual change is not well served by the language of science, which emphasizes clarity and supposedly unpolluted fact. We tend to minimize surprise by defining away changes we can't trace through physical processes. The process of discomfort and metamorphosis that characterizes accepting the invitation to change is short-circuited by ruling such metamorphosis out of bounds as meaningless talk.

This loss is especially clear when we consider the loss of rites of passage and initiation in the modern West. "If we do not birth and die ritually, we will do so technologically, inscribing technocratic values in our very bones. Technology without ritual (or worse, technology as ritual) easily degenerates into knowledge without respect. And knowledge without respect is a formula for planetary annihilation. It matters greatly not only *that* we birth and die but *how* we birth and die."[7] The loss of ritual strands modern people without a powerful vehicle for going through change, and the power of what is lost can be seen clearly in the fact that people often improvise and piece together such rituals at times of change to meet this need.

Modern religiosity, too, can short-circuit change. If the dominant logic of modernity leaves the options of materialism and fundamentalism, the second is just as poorly suited as the first to embrace the spiritual opportunity of change.

---

7. Ronald L. Grimes, *Deeply into the Bone: Re-Inventing Rites of Passage* (Berkeley: University of California Press, 2000), 13.

Fundamentalism stresses to the extreme the unchanging and objective nature of truth. Unchanging, bedrock truths are not amenable to being refined; the discomfort with one's understanding of the world that characterizes spiritual change is seen as a fall from knowledge, a loss of faith. The very grace that can work through challenging our concepts and experiences of God can only be seen as the withdrawal of grace.

Many Paths for Change

Accepting the invitation to change involves setting out on a new path, but the diversity of spiritual pathways complicates this process. We may know we no longer want to be on the path we are on, but which path should we follow? Where do we go for guidance in walking this path? Do we have to choose one source of wisdom to the exclusion of others? How can we find a path that is uniquely ours and still have help along the way? These questions are challenging because the process of accepting change inevitably involves many false starts and contradictions that require us to stick with a path in a discerning manner rather than bounce around from one solution to another as soon as we come up against a block.

Spiritual paths are comprised of a coherent web of ideas and practices,[8] and we must have perseverance to walk far enough down a path to see its internal logic so that we can continue to adjust our practices and improve. This is

---

8. Cf. MacIntyre, *After Virtue*.

best done with the support and accountability of friends—
not just contemporary ones, but the many friends from the
past that wisdom traditions can offer us. But many of us in
our contemporary situation find ourselves without such a
community of friends, and those who are blessed with them
often have multiple voices of wisdom being offered to them.

Diversity is not necessarily a hindrance to spiritual
maturity. Many voices can make harmony as well as noise.
Scholars have tended to focus on the latter. Theology and
sociology have given us many cautionary tales about people
who approach spiritual traditions through a kind of serial
dating with only minor investment, usually centered on their
own ego.[9] This critique has followed into examinations of the
"nones," who are seen as rather uninformed about religion
and subject to pursuing the cheap grace of comfort without
the costly grace of holiness. Spiritual friendship obviously
needs to be aware of the problems of superficial faith.

However, while there is danger in dabbling in many
traditions, spiritual companions might also consider ways
to appreciate the spiritual impulses that drive people to this
experimentation. Diversity can enhance spiritual growth by
providing a new light with which to see the world. Times
of spiritual change often challenge our well-worn language
and images of God. Encountering another tradition provides
the opportunity for talking about the Ultimate beyond our

---

9. See for example the discussion of "Sheilaism" in Robert N. Bellah, *Habits of the
Heart: Individualism and Commitment in American Life* (Berkeley: University of
California Press, 1985).

current vocabulary for it. I would suggest that it is as if our typical piety were confined to a two-dimensional plane and the ideas from another tradition were capable of lifting us into a third dimension, able to see things in new ways.

This is even more true of interpersonal relationships than of reading—with friends from other traditions, we don't have to pose to conserve our appearance of faithfulness or orthodoxy; we can be radically honest and listen to questions that our own Christian friends would not think to ask. But this kind of exercise requires practice, and it requires the virtues of humility, courage, peacefulness, respect, awe of the other, and holy envy that see beauty in other ways of believing.[10]

For a few, the encounter between traditions at times of change can become an invitation to serious multiple belonging, setting out on a journey along a pathway seen from many vantage points. The theologian Raimon Panikkar said of his journey: "I 'left' as a Christian, 'found myself' a Hindu, and I 'return' as a Buddhist, without having ceased to be a Christian."[11] Multiple belonging takes some care, and there are many kinds, for instance, familial (through an interreligious marriage) or asymmetrical (belonging to one religion while identifying with another).[12] It is also tricky

---

10. Edward Foley, *Theological Reflection across Religious Traditions: The Turn to Reflective Believing* (Lanham, MD: Rowman & Littlefield, 2015).

11. Raimon Panikkar, *The Intrareligious Dialogue* (New York: Paulist Press, 1978), 2.

12. Catherine Corneille, "Multiple Religious Belonging," in *Understanding Interreligious Relations*, ed. David Cheetham, Douglas Pratt, and David Thomas (Oxford: Oxford University Press, 2013).

to determine whether multiple belonging takes part in two or more traditions at the same time (and whether people in those traditions would recognize this participation) or creates something new (a Buddhapalian).[13] In all cases, it creates both opportunity and complex questions.

Responding to Change in Fluid Times

Fluidity is a wonderful metaphor for the inevitability of change. It can't be held, but it can be channeled. In these times, it is better for spiritual companions to focus on issues of process than those of prediction. We don't need to abandon models of spiritual development that can focus and guide our work, but we do need to realize that lifetimes of spiritual growth are likely to vary much more than ever before. Therefore, we need to hold our own models lightly, being willing to go with the flow of where the Spirit seems to be leading. Practices such as discernment are likely to be of more use to us than elaborate itineraries of the spiritual life.

In these ways, spiritual friendship can learn from other helping professions, such as career and vocational counseling. Recent theorists have noted that long-established models of career development no longer make sense given current economic patterns in which unpredictable circumstances can have a large impact on the ultimate unfolding of a career.

---

13. Ibid.

This realization has led to exploring chaos theory as a model for career development; there may be some principles that influence development, but these are highly sensitive to initial conditions and unusual circumstances.[14] Contexts matter more than individual traits.

Chaotic development, whether in career path or spiritual path, means that we cannot predict easily how a life will unfold, but we can help build skills to respond well at any point in that story. By focusing on people's unfolding stories, spiritual companions can help them claim their own voices to tell the story of their lives, place the challenges they encounter in the context of new stories, and be attentive moment by moment so that they can make the best decisions they can.[15]

Applying this model to spiritual friendship leads us to revisit the idea of stability, a dangerous task. A fluid concept of stability may collapse under its own weight compared to the wisdom of the past. There are many questions to answer, for instance: how essential is physicality and embodiment to true stability? Can stability be achieved through a sequence of commitment to different communities? Can it be virtual? What is gained and lost?

This exploration will undoubtedly take a great deal of time and the wisdom of many. That said, traditions already

---

14. R. G. L. Pryor and J. E. H. Bright, "Applying Chaos Theory to Careers: Attraction and Attractors," *Journal of Vocational Behavior* 71, no. 3 (2007): 375–400.

15. M. L. Savickas et al., "Life Designing: A Paradigm for Career Construction in the 21st Century," *Journal of Vocational Behavior* 75, no. 3 (2009): 239–50.

have the seeds of a response. In Christianity, for example, the Benedictine model of stability has been widely influential in recent writings on spiritual formation,[16] but there is much to be learned from the experiences of mendicant and missionary orders, such as the Dominicans, Franciscans, and the Jesuits.

For instance, at one key transition point in my spiritual life immediately after seminary, I found myself simply overwhelmed with my life and its responsibilities. I had a new child and had recently moved. The spirituality instilled in me from seminary that had served me so well—focused on the Daily Office and regular contemplative prayer—was not holding up, and I felt guilty and like a failure.

I had chosen a Carmelite spiritual director at this time because I thought these difficulties were signs of dryness, which obviously meant I was called to deeper contemplative prayer as described in the work of John of the Cross. Confounding all my expectations, this woman, who was herself dedicated to a life of silence and contemplation, suggested that I stop worrying and stop reading John of the Cross. Instead, she confronted me by pointing out that God had given me an infant to spend time in the presence of—an opportunity beyond most others for immense contemplation. She suggested that I give up any formal practices except something like the Ignatian Examen, reviewing where I had encountered God at the end of each day and how I had responded. In their place,

---

16. See for example Dorothy C. Bass and Craig R. Dykstra, *For Life Abundant: Practical Theology, Theological Education, and Christian Ministry* (Grand Rapids, MI: William B. Eerdmans, 2008).

she recommended a renewed attention to recalling that I am in God's presence throughout the day (borrowing from her own tradition's Brother Lawrence).

It is worth noting that she was not calling upon me to give up being rooted in spiritual community and the encounter with God. She was calling upon me to give up an itinerary that I thought led to God and instead accept God's gift of each moment with empty hands and gratitude. This is a core wisdom that is needed to respond to the invitation to change.

Fluid modernity forces us to hold lightly our itineraries for the spiritual life. It forces us to realize that spiritual stability is a gift and not something we can own or compel. It means that the spiritual question of accepting change is always in front of us. It means that it is better to think of stability as an orientation of the heart than a concrete rule of life. More important than any particular set of practices is a foundation of holy indifference, not tipping the balance in favor of any option, new or old, as we pray for the grace to see what fruits such decisions can bring.[17] Spiritual companions cannot rely too heavily on their models when working with people in the swirl of fluid modernity.

When our friends are confronted with an opportunity for spiritual change, we can help them by being prayerful and discerning companions in the moment, borrowing from chaplaincy's model of the "intimate stranger."[18] In times of

---

17. Ignatius, *Spiritual Exercises.*

18. Robert C. Dykstra, "The Intimate Stranger," in *Images of Pastoral Care: Classic Readings*, ed. Robert C. Dykstra (St. Louis, MO: Chalice Press, 2005).

upheaval, platitudes about God fall flat. More important than God talk at these moments of change is the practice of hospitality, honoring the basic needs of our friend and making room for the *Deus Absconditus* ("hidden God," Isaiah 45:15) that we experience in such moments. This process can take an uncomfortable amount of time, and our role as spiritual friends is often to help others persevere, holding faith for them, until a doorway to a new life opens.

Unfortunately, the doors that open are often strange and hard to see, especially given the modern penchant for reductionism and incontrovertible proof. We need practice in honing the spiritual senses so that we can perceive God's appearance. More than ever before, spirituality is not handed to us in reliable packages, and we must cultivate an incarnational worldview capable of finding God in all things—making our world a sanctuary instead of searching for a temple. In this work, spiritual friends can help others cultivate an attention for beauty and their moral passions, for these are often the places where God first appears, and the flatness of modern utilitarianism can drown them out.

But the work is not finished once we go through the doorway. Beauty and morality are indeed portals to the spiritual life,[19] but they can also become dead ends.[20] A true

---

19. Paul J. Deal, "Sanctification within the Middle Ground: A Narrative Phenomenology of Nature as Sacred" (PhD dissertation, Loyola University Maryland, 2015).

20. Søren Kierkegaard, *Stages on Life's Way*, trans. Walter Lowrie (New York: Schocken Books, 1967).

religiosity is no longer under our control or comprehension, and it is pursued for its own sake. Therefore, the path of accepting the invitation to change must increasingly be followed for its own intrinsic reasons, not extrinsic ones such as social or divine benefits.[21]

As indicated earlier, postmodern approaches to vocational counseling have noticed that while there are few stable things we can count on in our lives, we always have our story. Therefore, even in liquid modernity, accepting change calls for configuring the meaning of one's experience within the broader story of one's life. Christian spirituality offers the ideas of tradition and accountable community for making sense of our own story.[22] To find out the meaning of our own lives and how we live them each moment, we must be able to think about what it means to live well and to learn from those in the present and the past about how to do so. Therefore, despite the regularity of change, we are not to go forth alone.

As spiritual friends working with those facing change without roots, we can help them recognize and walk through thresholds into practicing community, even if sequential or virtual. This will force us to give up some of our long-held convictions about how church should look and lead us to examine other models of community. What is encouraging is that serious spiritual practice tends to re-create the basic structures

---

21. Gordon W. Allport, *The Individual and His Religion, a Psychological Interpretation* (New York: Macmillan, 1950).

22. MacIntyre, *After Virtue.*

of mentoring, classic texts, teaching, and practice, even if the content is quite different from traditional spirituality.[23]

These kinds of insights can be brought to the special case of multiple belonging in response to pluralism. What kind of multiple belonging it is matters. There is a difference between thoughtful engagement with multiple traditions and being a dilettante. When we examine some of the great figures who have sought to combine Christianity with another religion (such as Thomas Merton, Bede Griffiths, and Henri Le Saux), we notice certain features that distinguish their journeys from careless syncretism: their engagements did not arise from ignorance of their own tradition; they were aware of the need for intellectual and practical mastery of those religions they were exploring; they looked to integrate in experience, being formed and surprised; their faiths catalyzed one another for action; and they did not sidestep the tensions between the faiths.[24] Their goal was not "syncretism or synthesis, but symbiosis."[25]

The torrent of fluidity provides us with a unique spiritual opportunity: to be incapable of ignoring change. The important question for spiritual companions who stand with others in this situation is how to help them not only experience but accept change. Some very ancient wisdom can help us here, but it has to be wrestled with.

---

23. Bender, *New Metaphysicals*.

24. Peter C. Phan, *Being Religious Interreligiously: Asian Perspectives on Interfaith Dialogue* (Maryknoll, NY: Orbis Books, 2004).

25. Ibid., 75.

Questions for Discussion

1   This chapter notes the challenges that contemporary society poses to the idea of stability. What do you believe is essential to this spiritual virtue? What can be changed from culture to culture?

2   What examples can you give of when encountering a different tradition has allowed you to look at your tradition with fresh eyes? Was there anything about this situation that made it helpful rather than distracting?

3   What "portals" to the spiritual life have you encountered that might be surprising? What encouraged people to walk through them?

For Further Reading

Bass, Diana Butler. *Grounded: Finding God in the World—A Spiritual Revolution*. San Francisco: HarperOne, 2015. A journey through how contemporary spirituality can arise through engagement with the world, offering examples of thresholds to deeper spirituality that address the challenges of our times.

Knitter, Paul F. *Without Buddha I Could Not Be a Christian*. Oxford: Oneworld, 2009. A perceptive and intriguing account of one theologian's journey to integrated spirituality through pursuing multiple traditions.

Radcliffe, Timothy. *What Is the Point of Being a Christian?* New York: Burns & Oates, 2005. A look into what difference Christian spirituality makes to how we live life and how we might explain that difference to others.

CHAPTER 4

Suffering and the Spirit

FOR ALL ITS CONFUSION AND anxiety, embracing change can be exhilarating. There are many choices to be made, practices to pursue, new things to learn. We are being re-formed and renewed, and we want to throw ourselves into this process. But as in any love story, infatuation with God cannot last. The experiences and images of God we develop and cultivate inevitably dry up. The friends and organizations that defined our lives vanish. Trauma kicks our understandings of the world out from under us. This loss is agonizing, disorienting. We can't go back, since the very contexts that once defined our story would now mean something very different. We are tossed about in a stormy sea of doubt.[1] We don't know when or if help is coming. And we are powerless.

This spiritual moment is the Dark Night of which John of the Cross wrote. Our rigid ideas of what is sacred—idols that we use to contain God—are being refined. Therefore, despite the suffering, this kind of time can be an occasion of God's grace, for in depriving the soul of comfort and satisfaction, "God is freeing you from yourself and taking from you your own activity."[2] There is nothing for us to do; all is God here.

But we do have to respond. In the face of suffering and this passive purgation, we can respond with trust, perseverance, consent, and giving up efforts to force things to resolve.[3] These are the responses that a spiritual companion can foster, and we should notice that none of these involve thinking things through. In saying that suffering can be an occasion for spiritual growth, we run the risk of misunderstanding what is at stake. Too often, Christianity in particular has encouraged people to accept their oppression under this kind of pious logic. We should be clear that suffering is not to be desired or sought out. We must hope it is brief. It is not meant to be explained away or dismissed as a growth opportunity. Christians believe in following Jesus along the way of the cross, and the cross leads to real, cold, impotent, senseless death. That is the point. For Christians, God is in solidarity with those in the deepest

---

1. Shaia uses this image from Mark's Gospel as a visual for this stage.

2. John of the Cross, *The Collected Works of St. John of the Cross,* Kindle Ed. (Washington, DC: Institute of Carmelite Studies, 1979), Kindle Locations 9280–9282.

3. Ibid., Kindle Locations 8208–8210.

hell of suffering. Christ's victory over death does not come without the suffering of Good Friday and the silence of Holy Saturday. The spirituality of suffering may lead to Easter, but this period participates in the passion and death of Jesus, and it must be gone through, not preempted by facile theologies of glory. In time, all shall be well, but we mock suffering when we try to comfort others with facile words. The only response is to wait in solidarity. And the manner in which we undertake this vigil is shaped by our current times.

Suffering with Fluid Relationships

While I suggested that the fluid nature of modern relationships can force us into confronting the invitation to change, it makes it difficult to stick with change once we have accepted this invitation. Change and suffering go together, and fluidity makes suffering hard. It creates an infinitely revisable, low-commitment, low-friction way of interacting with others. It creates social circles based on affinity or brand. It creates shared spaces in which people don't have to interact with one another. In short, fluidity ensures that all of us are free to pursue our identity as we wish without interference from others. This means that when we encounter crisis, we are also likely to be left alone by others. In our society, people suffer alone together. This changes the spiritual dynamics of going through difficult times in fundamental ways.

Most spiritual traditions counsel that times of distress are when we need spiritual friends the most. We need the safety of a holding environment in which we can struggle to make meaning out of what is happening. For our faith to mature, we need others who can believe for us when we can no longer believe, and offer us new ways of coping when the old ways no longer work. We need the wisdom of a tradition that has dealt with these struggles before.

Instead, we find ourselves on our own. We may indeed have close friends who support us and even try to bear some of our burdens, but liquid relationships are often skittish about spirituality, which is, after all, a personal quest. It is easy to give up on the spiritual life or take a scattershot approach to try to find something that works. The problem is that to mature spiritually through suffering, we must go somewhere we have never been before on a road we do not know.[4] To walk in this darkness requires someone to lean on and the patience to see it through. "For the time being" relationships are not often up to the task. The bargain of liquid modernity is that you don't have to be Roman Catholic just because your mom was, but you also can't expect your Crossfit friends to be able to help you process your image of God when your mom dies.

Buying Normal

One of the ways that suffering can pose a spiritual opportunity is that it challenges our notions of self. Suffering

---

4. Ibid.

teaches us that we are not in control of all that happens to us. We are vulnerable. Bad things can and do happen to good people. But consumer capitalism is predicated upon the illusion of the self that is free to have what it wishes. Therefore, we are trained to see unhappiness as a technical problem to fix with the right treatment: pills, exercise, healthy eating, cognitive therapy, meditation, a vacation. Not only does this dynamic potentially short-circuit the wisdom that can only be learned through suffering, but no pill can fix vulnerability. It isn't something to be fixed. As Henri Nouwen points out, it is a basic part of the human condition, one that forces us to confront the contingency of our being.

> The truth is that a very large, if not the largest,
> part of our lives is passion. Although we all
> want to act on our own, to be independent
> and self-sufficient, we are for long periods of
> time dependent on other people's decisions. . . .
> We need people, loving and caring people, to
> sustain us during the times of our passion and
> thus support us to accomplish our mission.[5]

In passion, we are not in control. Our ego is challenged and chastened.

---

5. Henri J. M. Nouwen, *Adam: God's Beloved* (Maryknoll, NY: Orbis Books, 1997), 90–91.

Modern medicine is dedicated to giving us some semblance of control over our suffering. To sustain its marketability—not to mention get insurance reimbursement—modern medicine encourages the fiction that each person's suffering can be cured by appropriate diagnosis and treatment. In fact, some research suggests that spirituality is itself a helpful treatment for some problems. This approach turns a patient's body into a kind of very complex machine that can be regulated with the best empirically supported treatment. We are encouraged to believe that with enough time and resources, we can cure any ailment. It does not take a big step to conclude that embodiment and frailty themselves are the enemy, and this viewpoint is widespread—consider the appeal of uploading our consciousnesses into the cloud as a form of immortality. Solving these kinds of problems is what the scientific method is best at, and the suffering of countless millions has been reduced through the knowledge given to us in modern medicine. But this market-based logic limits medicine exactly where it can have spiritual significance.

The goal of treatment is to restore normal function. But "normal" is a slippery word. In scientific parlance, it is descriptive: normal is typical, average, the norm. But being normal has taken on a moral veneer. We not only want to be normal, but being abnormal is bad. There is a subtle denigration of the human worth of those who are not typical or healthy. The problem is that none of us are.

Controlling the Idea of Suffering

Modern philosophy and science encourage pernicious habits of thought that are a poor match for times of suffering. Modernity stresses clear and unshakable beliefs that no rational person would have reason to doubt. There need to be some fundamental ways to prove something is true. In this view, theological proofs can come through only two independent sources: rational reflection on the nature of deity or supernatural revelation. The result is a faith that tries to play by the rules of modern science. Its truth comes from a set of statements that correspond to "how things really are," a God's-eye view of the universe. Among its many flaws, this model tends to reduce faith to belief in a list of true things rather than faith as a coherent way of understanding and living. The result is theism, a theology based on propositions about God that can be "proven" to everyone. And in the face of suffering, theism creates atheism through its apparent contradictions. People can't be expected to believe six impossible things before breakfast.[6]

We don't have to study philosophers to see this effect. Research on religious coping has identified how a faith based on propositions can lead to spiritual crisis. When their beliefs are no longer self-evidently true to them, people enter

6. The White Queen, in Lewis Carroll, *The Annotated Alice: Alice's Adventures in Wonderland & Through the Looking-Glass* (New York: Norton, 2000).

spiritual crisis. They see God as angry with them, blame bad karma for their problems, doubt God's existence, and in short, rationalize something beyond the grasp of logic.[7]

The problem is that the spiritual response to suffering is not thought. Great spiritual traditions have long known this. As the monk John Climacus puts it, "Theology and mourning do not go together, for the one dissipates the other. The difference between a theologian and a mourner is that one sits on the professorial chair while the other passes his days in rags on a dungheap."[8] If the only choices are a theism that contradicts our experience or atheism, then atheism is clearly the more authentic spiritual choice. But perhaps these are not the only choices.

Seeing faith as a set of clear, fundamental assertions about the nature of reality encourages idolatry. In the words of the philosopher Jean-Luc Marion, "When a philosophical thought expresses a concept of what it then names 'God,' this concept functions exactly as an idol. It gives itself to be seen, but thus all the better conceals itself."[9] Our journey into the nature of reality just stops when we think we have a definitive answer.

---

7. See Kenneth I. Pargament, *Spiritually Integrated Psychotherapy: Understanding and Addressing the Sacred* (New York; London: Guilford, 2011), and Hye Sung Park, "Won Buddhist Coping in America among the First and Second Generation Korean Immigrant Population" (PhD dissertation, Loyola University Maryland, 2015).

8. John Climacus, *The Ladder of Divine Ascent*, trans. Colm Lubheid and Norman Russell (New York: Paulist Press, 1982), 139.

9. Jean-Luc Marion, *God without Being: Hors-Texte*, Kindle Ed. (Chicago: University of Chicago Press, 1991).

Underneath this rationalist approach to suffering is a strange minimizing of feeling and desire. By claiming to be untainted by bias and irrationality, modern philosophy betrays a kind of anxiety at its core. And emotions and desire are simply driven underground. God images are not just facts we believe; they are unconscious ways of relating to the universe.[10] Suffering confronts us with the reality that spirituality is not confined to the head, and our whole selves will be transformed. Modernity does not give us language to understand this process very well.

Many Paths through Suffering

The diversity of spiritual traditions also brings a complexity to suffering, for both good and ill. Knowing about other spiritual options can create a "grass is greener" temptation to end one's current journey and set out on another path. It is hard to hold on through struggle and darkness when there is another perfectly viable option available. The problem is that since spiritual maturity only comes through purgation, we never end up with a deeper faith, just a sequence of shallow ones.

That said, we should not avoid other traditions in times of suffering. Especially in the encounter between theist and nontheist faiths, such as Christianity and Buddhism, we can see

---

10. Ana-Maria Rizzuto, *The Birth of the Living God: A Psychoanalytic Study* (Chicago: University of Chicago Press, 1979).

people coming to unique, grace-filled insights. Encountering other faiths can be a way God purges us of "God" to let God appear. The language and practices of another faith, when explored with a wise spiritual companion, can reveal new aspects of God. In fact, when one is examining a faith that is not one's own, there is no pressure to "measure up" or prove what a good believer one is. One's spiritual baggage is set aside and a space is opened up for God to speak to us.

Being a Companion through Postmodern Darkness

Suffering is miserable. Suffering in postmodern society is miserable, isolating, and disorienting. Spiritual companions have one major gift to offer here: solidarity. Physical, loving presence. Not many words, and definitely not platitudes. We should remember that Job's comforters were especially keen on rationalizing his experience, so even if growth can come after suffering, it does very little good for us to offer explanations in lieu of encouragement and presence. I can't think of anyone who has been helped by being told that "God won't give you more than you can bear," and I can think of many for whom this kind of statement has been harmful.

Often, people going through the darkness of suffering need help in learning how to keep their thoughts from getting stuck in negative feedback loops and in gaining energy to engage with the world. Believing that grace can come despite this suffering is not an excuse for ignoring the knowledge and wisdom of the mental health professions. The patterns of thought that accompany depression, anxiety, and anger make spiritual growth difficult at best. In the language of Buddhism, these kinds of thoughts are poisons that need to be counteracted if we are to move toward enlightenment.[11] Therapy can be necessary for the spiritual life.

In attending to the spiritual dynamics of suffering, companions can keep in mind the wisdom of John of the Cross in his explanation of the Dark Night: "Since these dense darknesses have deprived her of all satisfaction—love alone . . . is what guides and moves her, and makes her soar to God in an unknown way along the road of solitude."[12] Love guides us up the secret stair through suffering to new life. But this statement needs to be parsed.

I've read this passage during a period of spiritual struggle and come away with the impression that it was a kind of cruel joke, that somehow God required a kind of heroic act from me that I was not capable of. But in Christian theology, love is not a personal possession. God is the kind of love that is ecstatic, not contained to one person. Christianity holds that others' love can inhabit us through solidarity in the Holy Spirit. This is exactly how the crucified Christ cannot be

---

11. The three root *kleśas* of greed, hate, and delusion are seen as the cause of all unwholesome dynamics that keep us mired in the pain of this existence.

12. John of the Cross, Kindle Locations 9790–9793.

conquered by death—the bond of love within God, the Holy Spirit, cannot be erased, and it is not dependent on the will of one person. If love is the pathway through suffering, then it is the love Christianity talks about as communion in the mystical body of Christ, believing and hoping for us when we cannot, testifying that there is a pathway beyond.

Therefore, to follow the Spirit during times of suffering, we need to be held. This is a challenge for a spiritual companion. There is the fear of contagion, of being cut off from the community, of venturing out too far from our spiritual home and losing the way back. The stakes are high, especially since poor spiritual companionship can exacerbate problems. When God is taking the soul in a new direction, the spiritual companion needs to be able to recognize this and not force a return to old ways of experiencing God.

It is also the case that post-traumatic growth tends to be associated with those who see their religion as a quest or intrinsically worth pursuing rather than as a source of benefits.[13] These individuals tend to be able to have their spiritual understandings and practices evolve, whereas those who see religion just as a way to be good or to avoid hell tend to cling more to spiritual resources that are not up to the task. Spiritual companions can make a difference by helping people recognize that faith is not something that we possess, to be kept in the locked box of the heart until we need it. We should

---

13. Mary Beth Werdel and Robert J. Wicks, *Primer on Posttraumatic Growth: An Introduction and Guide* (Hoboken, NJ: John Wiley & Sons, 2012), 8.

expect that if our faith comes from God, our understanding of it will grow and change.

Normalizing Vulnerability

Modern consumerism and medicine can see vulnerability as something to be fixed or solved. This can create a false sense of self that insulates us from growth. However, reengaging vulnerability is spiritually tricky. For instance, some well-intentioned Christian reflections on disability can trivialize it.[14] They can operate out of pity, placing the "whole" person as a hero and reducing those with disabilities to virtuous sufferers who are there for others' edification. Or in recognizing a shared vulnerability, they can ignore the real structures of injustice that face individuals with specific disabilities.

Spiritual companions can help others recognize that vulnerability and dependence are part of human nature, the *imago Dei* talked about in Christian theology. The essence of being human is not independence or rational deliberation, but being a dependent person loved into being.[15] Therefore, our encounters through suffering with our fundamental woundedness and loneliness can give us the ability to accept these and make room for encountering others.[16] But as Henri

---

14. Thomas E. Reynolds, *Vulnerable Communion: A Theology of Disability and Hospitality* (Grand Rapids, MI: Brazos Press, 2008).

15. Ibid.

16. Henri J. M. Nouwen, *Reaching Out: The Three Movements of the Spiritual Life* (New York: Random House, 1986).

Nouwen noted, woundedness can be a source of healing only if it is "carefully tended."[17] Therefore, collaborating with others in the healing professions is essential when companioning others through dark times.

Reintroducing Apophaticism

When spirituality adopts the anxieties and frameworks of modernity, it ironically tends to trivialize the spirit and experience[18] in favor of articulating truths and making sure that people know them. This tendency makes the dark night of the spirit into a time of rejecting or re-affirming these fundamental truths. The obvious problem with this framework is that it makes spiritual darkness a time for theological disputation. Spiritual companions should resist the temptation to engage in apologetics at these times. They should also resist the modern tendency to dismiss certain beliefs as silly, old-fashioned nonsense. God is the director during these times, and God will bring new spiritual realities into existence quite well without our intellectual engagement. The goal should be patience; we certainly can and should explore our theological

17. Henri J. M. Nouwen, *The Wounded Healer: Ministry in Contemporary Society* (Garden City, NY: Doubleday, 1972).

18. In her systematic theology Sarah Coakley explores this phenomenon at length, suggesting both pentecostalism and contemplative spirituality as potential paths of resistance to modernism. See *God, Sexuality and the Self: An Essay "On the Trinity"* (Cambridge: Cambridge University Press, 2013).

questions and emerging new ideas, but we should be discerning in how ready we are to latch onto them.

The Jesuit theologian Karl Rahner gives an eloquent statement about how spiritual darkness works:

> What can be taken from you is never God. . . . Don't be shocked at the loneliness and desertedness of your inner prison, which seems to be filled only with powerlessness and hopelessness, with tiredness and emptiness! . . . If you don't run away from despair, if in your despair at the idols of your life up till now, idols of body or mind, beautiful and honorable idols, idols you called God—if in this despair you don't despair of the true God, if you can stand firm in this way (this is already a miracle of grace), then you will suddenly become aware that you're not in fact buried alive after all, that your prison is shutting you off only from what is null and finite, that its deathly emptiness is only a disguise for an intimacy of God's, that God's silence . . . is filled by the Word without worlds, by Him who is above all names, by Him who is all in all. And his silence is telling you that He is here.[19]

---

19. Karl Rahner, *The Need and Blessing of Prayer*, trans. Harvey Egan (Collegeville MN: Liturgical Press, 1997), 8.

Rather than seeing spiritual crisis as a time of affirming or discounting tenets of faith, we need to recover a rich sense of apophatic spirituality. Apophatic theology is often presented as a way of approaching God through denial as opposed to kataphatic theology, which approaches God through affirmation. But it is more than that. One of the sources of Christian apophaticism, the (unfortunately named) Pseudo-Dionysius, takes pains to remind his readers that we must also negate the negations.[20] We are not simply moving to a time of saying "God is not that," but one of also saying "but God is also *not* not that."

Spiritual darkness is not an experience of darkness, of nothing or negation.[21] It is the experience we have when we are blinded by the brilliance of the overflowing reality of God. In the dark night, we encounter a "ray of darkness"[22] and experience a phenomenon that is saturated and overflowing with infinite meanings which we can't unify.[23] It forces us to move past theism and the expectation of what god is in favor of encountering the stranger that is God, and the negation of the theism we had. But a spirituality of apophaticism is not simply atheistic either. The theologian Richard Kearney describes this third option as anatheism: "Ana-theos, God

---

20. Pseudo-Dionysius, "The Mystical Theology," in *Pseudo-Dionysius: The Complete Works*, trans. Colm Luibhéid (New York: Paulist Press, 1987).

21. Denys Turner, *The Darkness of God: Negativity in Christian Mysticism* (Cambridge: Cambridge University Press, 1995).

22. Pseudo-Dionysius, "Mystical Theology," Ch. 1.

23. Marion, *God without Being*.

after God. . . . Another idiom for receiving back what we've given up as if we were encountering it for the first time. . . . In short, another way of returning to a God beyond or beneath the God we thought we possessed."[24]

Spiritual companions need the ability to recognize the emergence of new pictures of God beyond the ones theism tends to hold dear. Modern emphasis on reason and logic has promoted the "alls": God is all-powerful, all-knowing, all-good. The problem with these images is that they encourage a kind of complacency in speaking about God. God is big, good, powerful, etc., just like us, except infinitely more so. The reality is that we literally don't know what we are saying when we say God is good. Goodness really applies to God, and what we call goodness is only analogous to it. When we minimize the strangeness of God, we end up with God as an idea, or watchmaker, or guy, incapable of compassion. But the scriptures of Judaism and Christianity have a great deal of language about the concern and suffering of God that seems incompatible with the alls. This language is what makes God living; humankind is God's perpetual concern, and God is not indifferent and self-sufficient.[25] Knowledge that there are different—indeed infinite—ways to describe God can allow an attentive spiritual companion to facilitate a friend's journey when there are glimpses of these new possibilities.

---

24. Richard Kearney, *Anatheism: Returning to God after God* (New York: Columbia University Press, 2010), 3.

25. Abraham Joshua Heschel, *The Prophets* (New York: Harper & Row, 1962).

Questions for Discussion

1 What images of God do you find most appealing? Which bother you? How do you engage in spiritual friendship with someone whose images do not align with your own? Is any image as good as any other?

2 Do you think that atheism can be a more authentic spiritual stance than theism? Under what conditions? What kind of atheism?

3 Who has helped you most in times of suffering? What did they do? What didn't they do?

For Further Reading

Chödrön, Pema. *When Things Fall Apart: Heart Advice for Difficult Times.* Boston: Shambhala, 1997. A classic of contemporary Buddhist spirituality that speaks directly to how to mature through suffering.

Halík, Tomáš. *Patience with God: The Story of Zacchaeus Continuing in Us.* New York: Doubleday, 2009. Having served as a secretly ordained priest during communist rule in the Czech Republic, Halík examines the spiritual longings at work in atheism and what they might have to say to Christian faith.

Williams, Rowan. *The Edge of Words: God and the Habits of Language.* New York: Bloomsbury, 2014. This book, based on Williams's Gifford Lectures, explores how the unusual features of speech and the limits of language can inform our metaphysics, with many implications for apophatic theology.

CHAPTER 5

Receiving Joy

RECEIVING JOY PROBABLY DOES not sound like much of a task. But that is its intoxicating glamor, not its substance. If we think about it a bit more, we remember that times of joy have often stretched us in our spiritual lives: "We prayed that our yearning, outstretched hand would be met by a firm, answering grip that would lead us ashore. That is not what we get, though. We get infinitely more. Yet no step we have taken, nor prayer we have prayed, could have prepared us for the wonder of this moment."[1] Searching for happiness, we get wonder. As we have been

---

1. Shaia, *Hidden Power*, 152.

taken to a spring of grace, upwelling joy enlarges our souls and brings us beyond our understanding.

This means that there is actually a danger in receiving joy—thinking that the lack of effort on our part means that we have mastered it: "Our insights are not yet fully mature, *although they feel so.* In fact, the world is full of people who reached the point of ephiphany and immediately rushed out to share their supposed wisdom, and instead created only havoc. Wisdom is a much longer journey."[2] In the language of John's Gospel, we are called to abide, to linger and become absorbed in the presence. The bliss that marks joy's arrival is not its substance. Complete joy transforms us and makes us participants in God's own activity.

This is an important warning that we see across spiritual traditions. We can catalog and analyze states of ecstasy, but these are only preludes to true awakening. Times of joy are a wonderful opportunity for being a spiritual friend, but they are risky, since we can become convinced that the power of our teaching is responsible, not God. We need to avoid imposing our preferred practices on those in this moment and see where God is leading. Otherwise, we can become a source of spiritual interference, someone jerking the canvas while the master is painting.[3]

---

2. Ibid., 153.

3. This image and the advice to the director are found in John of the Cross, "Living Flame of Love," in *Collected Works*.

Flow

Interference is already constant in our lives. Fluidity means that we are always revising what we think will make us happy. Instead of steadily accumulating the "dream" piece by piece—a management position, 2.5 kids, and a suburban McMansion—we are always tempted by some new and better vision. This is on purpose. Desire for a specific kind of happiness, an achievement, a thing, stops somewhere. Fluidity encourages wishing instead of desire for—the search for pleasure no longer has to contend with any possible reality we could achieve. There are no norms, no "Joneses" to keep up with.[4] Just never-satisfied wishing for more. Which capitalism will gladly sell us.

The sinister thing about replacing desire with wish is that it mimics the wisdom of faith traditions about the pursuit of happiness. "You have made us for yourself Almighty God, and our hearts are restless until they rest in you"[5]—Augustine's wisdom about how we continually frustrate the search for God by resting in created pleasures sounds almost the same as what fluidity fosters. The same could be said of the Buddhist cultivation of nonjudgmental detachment from things that are impermanent. But in both cases, there is an additional aspect—both traditions base their wisdom on a conviction

---

4. Bauman, *Liquid Times*, Kindle Location 1660.
5. Augustine of Hippo, *Confessions*, trans. Maria Boulding (Hyde Park, NY: New City Press), 1.

that how things really are is incapable of being grasped, and yet existence is a continual gift from that incomprehensible source. Fluidity promises an infinity of more of the same.

Spirituality and fluidity share imagery for joy, but they differ in how they understand infinity. In Christian mysticism, the infinity of God is not an endless amount of more objects as infinite wishing has it. The infinity of God is qualitatively different, which means that we not only change continually, that change is a deeper and deeper realization of what is. A seminal figure in Christian mysticism, Gregory of Nyssa, provides an amazing image of what this looks like. Gregory is known for his doctrine of *epektasis*—endless progression:

> This truly is the vision of God: never to be satisfied in the desire to see him. But one must always, by looking at what he can see, rekindle his desire to see more. Thus, no limit would interrupt growth in the ascent to God, since no limit to the Good can be found nor is the increasing of desire for the Good brought to an end because it is satisfied.[6]

Rather than turning from one thing to another and another in the vanity of finding some new diversion, spirituality is drawn beyond its object, because its current vision kindles a desire to see more. We encounter God through the beauty of creation, and that beauty draws us inside itself to a deeper

---

6. Gregory of Nyssa, *The Life of Moses*, trans. Abraham Malherbe (New York: Paulist Press, 1978), 116.

knowledge, the ever-more of God. Rather than wandering the desert from oasis to oasis, the spiritual life happens when God places us at the wellspring and we drink more and more deeply from the source.

By contrast, fluid joy is captured well in its cognate, "flow." Flow is the state we experience when an activity has a perfect balance of being challenging and interesting. During flow, we are totally engrossed and time seems to fly.[7] Flow is ideally suited to fluidity: it can be encountered on the fly, in almost every setting, and it does not need to take lots of preparation or time. Psychologists and management consultants have seized upon this idea as a way to promote well-being in our busy world.

The concept of flow exhibits many of the ways in which the spirituality of joy is impacted. It is an individual peak experience. In some ways, that is not a problem, since fluid relationships mean that we don't have people to share more than the most basic levels of joy with. It is fleeting and seductive and portable. And we move on from it. To use the language of John's Gospel alluded to earlier, we don't abide.

Technological Utopias

When everything is a commodity, joy can be purchased. The purpose of much of modern science is to make sure that those purchases are reliable. We seek knowledge not so

7. Mihaly Csikszentmihalyi, *Finding Flow: The Psychology of Engagement with Everyday Life* (New York: Basic Books, 1997).

much for knowledge itself, but to be able to achieve our goals through the manipulation of nature. The result is the search for the pill, the device, the technology that will make things exactly as we would like them, which is assumed to be the basis for happiness. We can then sell those happiness widgets, which efficiently distributes them.

There are many reasons to worry about subjecting science to the commodification of happiness, not least of which is that what appears to make some people happy is the efficient exploitation and even slaughter of others. But try as we might to keep this critique in mind, the promise of technological utopias are too difficult to resist, and after all, it keeps the economy going. Technologists and futurists talk about a future in which we can become immortal or omniscient through science. One prominent insider to the tech industry suggests that "what we are seeing is a new religion, expressed through an engineering culture. . . . Technologists are creating their own ultramodern religion, and it is one in which people are told to wait politely as their very souls are made obsolete."[8]

This is a very specific take on happiness, rooted in the "device paradigm"[9] spoken about in chapter 1. In this paradigm, technology promises to take away everyday difficulties and make us happy through producing devices for those purposes. A device provides us a desired commodity

---

8. Jaron Lanier, *Who Owns the Future?*, Kindle ed. (New York: Simon & Schuster, 2013), Kindle Location 3029.

9. Borgmann, *Power Failure*.

with minimal effort, hiding all the complexities of the natural resources, human labor, and knowledge that allow it to work. Over time, these complexities become more and more hidden as we have gone from developing film to looking at our phone's touchscreen. The paradigmatic device is a switch—we don't need to understand or even think about how it works. It simply turns something on when we flip it.

In the end, then, commodified happiness reduces spirituality to the flip of a switch or taking a pill. The problem is that anything that can be achieved through unlimited quantities of drugs is probably not true happiness.

Incomplete Joy

If happiness is not simply a kind of perpetual good mood, then what is it? To think about this question, I often ask my students to consider what would happen were neuroscience to create a perfect brain regulator. What would be the purpose of psychotherapy in this world? Most of them would agree that something like therapy would still have a place, that this device would not replace the kind of growth that can come through mutual, caring relationship. But if I press them to think about what support for their opinion they have in the scholarly literature, there is usually a pause in the discussion—then they realize that it depends on which literature.

Psychotherapy is a wonderful field in which to consider how our modern focus on control and objectivity impacts our ideas of happiness. The field is split against itself: The dominant perspective embraces the ideal of psychology as an natural science bordering biology. In this paradigm, psychotherapy utilizes empirically supported best practices derived from progress made in understanding the mind and emotions. The "loyal opposition" sees psychology as an interpretive science bordering on philosophy. In this case, psychotherapy is seen as a talking cure that comes from helping individuals reshape their stories and relationships to live in a better, more authentic way.

These two approaches roughly correspond to approaches to happiness labeled *hedonic* and *eudaimonic*.[10] The hedonic approach insists that the only accurate way to talk about happiness is to focus on what can be empirically measured: the balance of positive and negative emotions, and satisfaction with life.[11] The eudaimonic approach takes the view that happiness is a life well-lived, characterized by certain virtues and practices. Of these two, only hedonism matches modern priorities: creating happiness devices through objective control. Virtues and practices don't lend themselves well to being measured or isolated from their context. It is not surprising that people seeking spiritual growth in our culture find happiness hard to grasp. Good mood and satisfaction

---

10. R. Ryan and E. Deci, "On Happiness and Human Potentials: A Review of Research on Hedonic and Eudaimonic Well-Being," *Annual Review of Psychology* 52 (2003): 141–66.

11. The research literature refers to this set of variables as "subjective well-being," and it has been the most dominant way for exploring the psychology of happiness empirically.

with life are important, maybe even necessary, for happiness, but they usually aren't all that people are searching for.

Spirituality seems to require a eudaimonic perspective. Consider the Farewell Discourse in John's Gospel: In the midst of it, Jesus says to his disciples that he has spoken these words "so that my joy may be in you, and that your joy may be complete."[12] What does this complete joy look like? The disciples are told that Jesus is the way to the Father. They are to bear fruit through adhering to Jesus, the vine. They are told to love one another as Jesus has loved them. They are told to abide in that love. They are told that while they may be persecuted, he will send the Comforter to be with them and complete his work. He prays for their unity and sanctity, that they may be united with him and the Father.

This complete joy has no description of mood, but repeated descriptions of the life that embodies it. If anything, good mood is secondary to it—there will be a Comforter, but in response to the difficulty of persecution. And at the center of this concept of joy is self-giving: laying down one's life for one's friends. A thick idea of happiness provides an antidote to the unbridled consumption and use of the world's resources that hedonism implies. Merton tells us that

> to seek happiness is not to live happily.
> Perhaps it is more true to say that one finds
> happiness by not seeking it. The wisdom that

---

12. John 15:11.

teaches us deliberately to restrain our desire
for happiness enables us to discover that we
are already happy without realizing the fact.[13]

Unfortunately, this wisdom about happiness runs counter to the ethos of control and objectivity that modern thought encourages. Joy is received; it involves giving up control. It is a way of life; it can't be thought of without being embodied in some definite tradition.

Whose Joy?

A eudaimonic understanding of joy may be richer, but it creates a problem in a diverse society. Quite simply, whose idea of joy do we live into? There may be some overlap between what different faiths envision the good life to be, but the deepest ideas of joy are the ones most deeply embedded in each faith's traditions and practices. As with the other movements of the spiritual life, diversity provides both opportunities and challenges for receiving joy.

The challenges are easy to see. If joy is the gift of being able to lead the good life, it will take time to develop. The diversity of spiritual paths can provide a distraction here. It would be as if we were finally getting good at Japanese and we started exploring Sanskrit. Sanskrit is not bad, but we will

---

13. Thomas Merton, *Thoughts in Solitude*, Kindle ed. (New York: Farrar, Straus & Cudahy, 1958), Kindle Location 1619.

miss out on the new way of seeing the world that Japanese has given us. Again, the image of moving the painting while the master is at work provides a good description. God is creating something beautiful, but we have to sit still for it to emerge.

We also need a spiritual home in which to cultivate that emerging life. Practices of faith are not individual activities. Diversity can tempt us to try to live in several different communities, and at some point, we must make a commitment to growing through fidelity to one of them.

That said, diversity doesn't have to be seen as just an unfortunate distraction from spiritual maturity. While the moment of receiving joy is one that draws us most deeply into our own tradition, the existence of other traditions reminds us that our picture is not complete, even if we feel especially enlightened. Seeing others deeply committed to their faith practices can give us new perspectives on ours. It is worth noting that the most productive interfaith exchanges tend to be between those who are mature in their faiths, where the encounter with the other is not a distraction or a danger but another aspect of the illumination that is happening.

Abiding in Postmodern Joy

The spiritual life is meant to lead us into times of joy. The problem is that we often have a truncated idea of what joy is. Contemporary trends encourage us to see joy as a sequence of fleeting ecstasies, which we can make more frequent if we use the right program or product—and there are a world of such products out there to try. Joy becomes something we can have anytime, anywhere—in fact, the ideal postmodern joy would be in pill form.

What if true joy were not a pill, but a fruit?[14] Then joy would not be something we have, but something that ripens in an organic, unpredictable process. Consider Rilke's advice on poetry:

> Being an artist means: not numbering and counting, but ripening like a tree, which doesn't force its sap, and stands confidently in the storms of spring, not afraid that afterward summer may not come. It does come. But it comes only to those who are patient, who are there as if eternity lay before them, so unconcernedly silent and vast. I learn it every day of my life, learn it with pain I am grateful for: patience is everything![15]

Cultivating fruit requires patience. It also is inextricably rooted in the relationships between the gardener, the earth, the sky, and God's grace. There are no tree machines or programs. And synthetic joy is about as attractive as synthetic peaches—perhaps we will have a peach in pill form, but I hope we won't settle for eating it that way.

---

14. As Paul says in Galatians 5:22.

15. Rainer Maria Rilke, *Letters to a Young Poet*, trans. Stephen Mitchell (New York: Vintage Books, 1984), 24.

Taking this image further, it is worth going back to John's Gospel and the concept of abiding. In John's Gospel, abide (*meno*) and its derivatives describe resting in loving union with God, a taste of the life to come.[16] The complex overtones of this word can be seen in the image of the vine and branches,[17] in which Jesus uses the term "abide" ten times in ten verses. Just as it is hard to distinguish where the vine ends and the branches begin, when we abide in Jesus the vine, we enter into intimate union with him in love. With language strongly suggestive of the Eucharist,[18] we absorb into our inmost being his words and his commands, we become his friend, and we bear fruit. It is in abiding that we can respond to the opportunities and challenges of postmodern joy, for in abiding in the love of Christ, we encounter a Trinitarian form of joy that is self-giving, dwelling among our physical world, lived out in fundamental practices of prayer and service.

Focal Realities

To counter the device paradigm of joy, we can learn from Albert Borgmann's concept of the "focal things."[19] Whereas devices are disposable delivery systems for product without

---

16. Thomas L. Brodie, *The Gospel According to John: A Literary and Theological Commentary* (New York: Oxford University Press, 1993).

17. John 15:1–10.

18. Brodie, *The Gospel According to John*.

19. Borgmann, *Power Failure*.

context, focal things engage our whole selves, body and mind. Focal things live in the world of time and space; they cannot be separated from the nexus of natural and cultural relationships surrounding them. They cannot be simulated or turned on and off. Therefore, they demand patience, endurance, skill, and resolute practice, shaping our character. Rather than distracting us from the world, they command that we engage the particularities of our setting. If postmodern joy wants to be a pill, focal things show that what postmodernity is asking for is addiction and illusion.

It should be a cause for hope to realize that the quest for focal things is all around us. Those who are on a serious quest to live authentically seem to have intuited that happiness is more than good feelings. Churchgoers are pursuing the focal things through richly incarnational worship and ancient ritual. Runners are pursuing focal things through marathons. We see focal things at the center of activities as diverse as brewing, gardening, yoga, cooking, and sewing, all of which are increasing in popularity. All of these give great joy, but only through patient abiding in that activity. Spiritual friendship can sometimes consist in helping people direct their interests into some of these activities.

Joy as a Way of Life

But how do these activities fit together into a good life? Here, we can augment Borgmann's insights with those of Alasdair MacIntyre, whose theory of human flourishing is also focused on practices that must be carefully cultivated in real, embodied settings with others.

For MacIntyre, practices are cooperative, complex activities in which people strive to achieve standards of excellence, to gain the "internal goods" that can be achieved only through the practice, and to expand human abilities and wisdom.[20] Practices take practice, and they cannot be pursued alone. They require coaching in how to do them well. And they provide joy, but only through persisting in them.

Practices are done in the context of our lives. Their meaning comes from their place in our own stories and histories. Therefore, not every practice is meant for every person or every season of life. Our emerging story forces us to think of what and when we are called to do in each circumstance. And this means that discernment becomes a fundamental spiritual need. To live a life of joy, we must learn to pay attention to how God wishes us to live.

Finally, if true happiness and the joy that accompanies it is a way of life, we cannot avoid engaging with what tradition says about what are the necessary practices of such a life. Tradition in this sense is living "an historically extended, socially embodied argument, and an argument precisely in part about the goods which constitute that tradition."[21] We cannot pursue a way of life without wrestling with the wisdom of the past. And in a

---

20. MacIntyre, *After Virtue*.
21. Ibid., 222.

diverse spiritual environment, our conversation partners are potentially so many that we have to prioritize listening to those whose form of life has the most to say to our own.

With MacIntyre's insights, we can see that to abide and mature in postmodern joy, we must help one another engage in three fundamental tasks of spiritual friendship. We must encourage serious practice in spiritual disciplines that are seen not as means to an end, but an end in themselves. We must help one another recognize through exercises of discernment, such as those of the Ignatian and Quaker traditions, the specific shape of the good life to which we are called. This discernment requires patient attention and a willingness to keep from predetermining the outcome. Finally, we must share what we have learned from the classics of our traditions and help one another make spiritual friends across the ages.

These fundamental tasks can be pursued in many settings, but in Christian spirituality, the central one is liturgy, in which we enter briefly into a taste of God's reign and practices of love are miraculously opened up to us.

Counterfeit Joys of Privilege

A final component of abiding in postmodern joy is the cultivation of critical consciousness. Too often, what we take as the "good life" is something available only to those with the leisure and resources to pursue it. Practices like meditation, brewing, and even "honoring sabbath" are often reliant upon the efficiency and free time received at the cost of those who have no control over their work schedules. When we measure spiritual maturity by volume of practices, we foster a revival of the old heresy of Pelagianism, in which we think that we are ourselves responsible for our self-betterment, diet, environmentalism, and any other virtues we uphold, minimizing grace, context, and the resources that make them possible. Abiding in joy is not the same as lingering in privilege.

Therefore, spiritual friendship must include helping one another raise this consciousness and empowering those who are oppressed to find their voices and tell their own story of what joy is. We must question the ways in which joy is packaged and sold. Sometimes, this is an easy task. There are routes to "happiness" being sold that are so decadent that any outside perspective would see their faults. But most counterfeit joys are not like the recent story in the *New York Times* about models in New York using liquid nitrogen baths to enhance their well-being.[22] Too often, we can be seduced by what Buddhism calls the "near enemies" of the good—things that seem virtuous on their surface, but end up disconnecting us from true happiness.

These small perversions of goodness are difficult to see, especially when our life circumstances do not place their burdens onto us. This is why we must heed Scripture's repeated calls to see the world in solidarity with those who

---

22. Paul Sullivan, "Getting Workaholics to Stop and Recharge," *New York Times*, Aug. 21, 2015. http://nyti.ms/1Jaj171.

are materially poor and vulnerable. This solidarity is not an intellectual exercise. As the theologian Gustavo Gutiérrez noted, "Solidarity is not with 'the poor' in the abstract but with human beings of flesh and bone. Without love and affection, without—why not say it?—tenderness, there can be no true gesture of solidarity."[23] Spiritual friends can help one another take the risk of entering into these relationships, especially as they are encountered in eucharistic community.

Complete joy does not come in a flash of the sublime, a self-improvement project, or a comfortable life. True joy comes when we abide—when we intently, sustainedly, vulnerably receive love. And as we see in John's Gospel, to love is to give of one's self. In our contemporary situation, it may be that this aspect of joy is the most countercultural. A joyful life is one that partakes in the self-giving of Christ, "who, though he was in the form of God, did not regard equality with God as something to be exploited, but emptied himself."[24] Joyful people are not those who have the most fun; they are the ones who through emptying of self bring life to others.

---

23. Gustavo Gutiérrez, *We Drink from Our Own Wells: The Spiritual Journey of a People* (Maryknoll, NY: Orbis Books, 1984).

24. Phil. 2:6–7.

Questions for Discussion

1 Do you agree that spirituality must have a eudaimonic conception of joy? Why or why not?

2 To what extent do you think that scientific research can uncover what makes us happy? What kind of knowledge of this research does a spiritual companion need to have?

3 How can we breach the topic of privilege in spiritual companionship? What are the first things that we must learn in order to develop a critical consciousness about how our spirituclity reflects our social context?

For Further Reading

Bass, Dorothy C., and Craig R. Dykstra, eds. *For Life Abundant: Practical Theology, Theological Education, and Christian Ministry*. Grand Rapids MI: Eerdmans, 2008. A collection of essays examining how MacIntyre's philosophy of practice can be applied to practical theology.

McFague, Sallie. *Blessed Are the Consumers: Climate Change and the Practice of Restraint*. Minneapolis: Fortress Press, 2013. A look at the relationship between happiness and the practice of restraint, offering historical paradigms of how this spirituality can be lived out.

Turkle, Sherry. *Alone Together: Why We Expect More from Technology and Less from Each Other*. New York: Basic Books, 2011. A critical examination of how the technological paradigm promises happiness and changes human relationships in the process.

CHAPTER 6

Maturing in Service

A S WE ABIDED IN THE experience of joy, we came to realize that true happiness lies in service to others. What seemed like a mountaintop experience of bliss has actually elevated us to a new plane of existence in which we see everything afresh. As Teresa of Ávila put it, "You may think that as a result the soul will be outside itself and so absorbed that it will be unable to be occupied with anything else. On the contrary, the soul is much more occupied than before with everything pertaining to the service of God; and once its duties are over it remains with that enjoyable company."[1] We don't worry about crashing down again

---

1. Teresa of Ávila, "Interior Castle," *Collected Works*, vol. 2. Kindle Locations 7324–7326.

because we have realized that both high and low are "charged with the power of God."[2]

Even so, it will take work to live in this new world. Shaia noted how unfortunate it is that this path is often neglected in popular psychological and spiritual writings, assuming that it will just happen. This is not the case. When our new convictions encounter the real world, they are tested. There is a temptation in the face of this anxiety to go backwards. To succeed, we must go slowly and practice living in this new world.

Great spiritual traditions make this point emphatically. In Christianity, authors such as Teresa remind us frankly that there is actually no separation between the "contemplative" life symbolized by Mary of Bethany and the "active" one of her sister Martha.

> This is what I want us to strive for, my Sisters; and let us desire and be occupied in prayer not for the sake of our enjoyment but so as to have this strength to serve. . . . Believe me, Martha and Mary must join together in order to show hospitality to the Lord and have Him always present and not host Him badly by failing to give Him something to eat. How would Mary, always seated at His feet, provide Him with food if her sister did not help her?[3]

---

2. Gerard Manley Hopkins, "God's Grandeur," *Poetry Foundation*, http://www.poetryfoundation.org/poem/173660.

3. Teresa of Ávila, "Interior Castle," Kindle Locations 7647–7652.

Even cloistered nuns like those whom Teresa was guiding should not think that the quiet of their prayer excuses them from service.

Moreover, as we go outside ourselves to love and serve others, we must remember that our transformation in joy does not mean that our spiritual formation is complete. Mahāyāna Buddhism highlights this reality in its doctrine of the bodhisattva. In this ideal, full Buddhahood is nothing short of the liberation of all sentient beings from suffering, not my own enlightenment. There is no such thing as a "lone Buddha."[4] From the perspective of wisdom, we now see that our own joy cannot be complete so long as there is suffering, for that would assume a difference between myself and others that is not real.

Therefore, Mahāyāna spirituality is focused on realizing the bodhisattva vow, which concludes, "Thus for everything that lives, As far as are the limits of the sky, May I be constantly their source of livelihood Until they pass beyond all sorrow."[5] Our own spiritual growth is meant to transform us into a source of healing for others. But this is not straightforward. Practice is required, and there are extensive spiritual exercises, such as *lojong* (mind training) focused on moving us beyond individual liberation to universal compassion. Reaching out in

4. Paul Williams, *Mahāyāna Buddhism: The Doctrinal Foundations*, 2nd ed. (New York: Routledge, 2008), 59.

5. Dalai Lama XIV and Śāntideva, *For the Benefit of All Beings: A Commentary on the Way of the Bodhisattva* (Boston: Shambhala, 2009), 32–33.

service is its very own moment of the spiritual life, not the corollary of receiving joy.

Serving a Fluid Neighborhood

Some of the same dynamics making it difficult to begin the spiritual journey also change the way in which we reach out for service. Love of neighbor looks different when many of our relationships are temporary, fragile, and negotiated. The resulting dynamic can both increase and decrease our care for others, but rarely will it lead to sustained change.

Consider how community in fluid times is usually a matter of choice. This dynamic means that we tend to create our own neighborhoods. Rather than the randomness of communities created by who moves in next door, there is a purposefulness to fluid communities. They are usually oriented around a shared life stage, interest, or practice. If we have wide-ranging interests, we might come into contact with very different people across our groups, but the life experiences they offer us match the range of our own.

Among other pursuits, I teach at a university and take part in a group that writes and performs choral music, several theology-related Facebook groups, a clergy group, a Cub Scout pack, and a group for parents of children with autism. I am greatly enriched by my friends in these groups, and I am fairly certain that some of the parents from scouts would never be interested in hanging out with the musicians. But they are all the kind of people that I would like to run into.

Groups that are chosen can be tremendously life-giving. In the life of these groups, I have seen acts of love in which people have comforted one another through loss, encouraged one another, or advocated for another's well-being. I encounter God in these times. However, there are relatively few times where we are called upon to offer real hospitality, to make room for someone truly Other who makes us stretch out of our comfort zones. So while fluidity provides us many opportunities to reach out in service, it offers few to mature through service.

Another important aspect of fluidity is that it tends to produce short-lived, ad hoc relationships. This means that as we reach out in service, we have many opportunities to get involved. There are 5K runs for charity, weekends working at Habitat for Humanity, cleanup days, and turns in the soup kitchen. In fact, if we care deeply about creating a way to serve others, fluidity minimizes the obstacles in our paths and fosters creativity by eliminating the inertia of established organizations. Temporary alliances can also be formed among groups that share a concern, but differ in some other major values. But even as it encourages starting ways to reach out, fluidity offers little to support seeing it through past a short-term goal. We must learn on our own to piece together a lifetime of service. Just as when we were starting down a spiritual path, fluidity gives us freedom but denies us guidance.

The implications of these dynamics for the spiritual life are clearest when we consider the distinction between charity and social justice. Fluidity can enhance opportunities for individually focused acts of love while making it hard to join together across divides in the pursuit of a good society. The problem is that both are essential to the spiritual life. Growth often comes when we have to show real hospitality to the stranger and when our worldviews are challenged. It rarely comes through just being nice.

Captive

Perhaps that is the way the current consumer economy needs it to be. Quite simply, when we are thinking about how others live, we are not paying attention to our own desires, and a consumer economy depends on us paying attention to our own desires so that it can distribute resources effectively. Therefore, consumer capitalism tends to reinforce the idea that each one of us is infinitely free to choose rationally between commodities that will make us a little happier. This economic model of human behavior is not necessarily evil; we need economic models to work toward functional societies. The problem from a spiritual perspective is that it distorts our self-understanding. We are not independent. We are not merely rational. The purpose of life is not consumption. We begin to misunderstand ourselves, and the false selves we create separate us from God and our neighbor.

Commodities also thwart the creativity of the spirit. Essential aspects of human life, like caring, mutual relationships, are not commodities. Yet, where the great spiritual traditions impel us to reach out through an ethic of self-giving, the only ethic available in a world of commodities is one of scarcity. We are encouraged to see goals such as care and justice as problems to be solved by efficient management and distribution of resources. We are asked to see how our desire to love can be put to good use, and the infinite possibilities of grace, which knows no scarcity, are caged. It is no wonder then that the single most difficult biblical commandment to follow in our time is to honor the Sabbath. The Sabbath requires, writes Heschel, that

> he who wants to enter the holiness of the day must first lay down the profanity of clattering commerce, of being yoked to toil. He must go away from the screech of dissonant days, from the nervousness and fury of acquisitiveness and the betrayal in embezzling his own life. He must say farewell to manual work and learn to understand that the world has already been created and will survive without the help of man. Six days a week we wrestle with the world, wringing profit from the earth; on the Sabbath we especially care for the seed of eternity planted in the soul. The world has our hands, but our soul belongs to Someone

> Else. Six days a week we seek to dominate the
> world, on the seventh day we try to dominate
> the self.[6]

This way of living is simply foolish from an economic perspective. And yet the testimony of Judaism is that it is precisely this attitude that makes life worth living. The God who led Israel out of slavery in Egypt is committed to a world that is about relationships, not commodities.[7] There is no such thing as a spirituality of service without relationship.

The challenge for spiritual companions is that we need to make an effort to break out of commodified living. If we were to live in ways that challenged its assumptions, it would stop working. Therefore, a key aspect of a consumer economy is that it masks its own dynamics. It does this by creating an unending flow of media that entertain us or call on us to express ourselves in trivial ways. With so much to do, we rarely have time or space enough to contemplate our lives and our society. And even if we are able to name this dynamic, we are so busy that we do nothing to change it.[8] The spiritual life has to find a way to break through this wall of distractions to start living differently.

---

6. Abraham Joshua Heschel, *The Sabbath: Its Meaning for Modern Man* (New York: Farrar, Straus and Giroux, 2005), 1.

7. Walter Brueggemann, *Sabbath as Resistance: Saying No to the Culture of Now* (Louisville, KY: Westminster John Knox Press, 2014), 6.

8. Michael Hardt and Antonio Negri, *Declaration* (New York: Argo-Navis Author Services, 2012), 16.

A World of Things

As discussed earlier, a key aspect of modern science[9] is its creation of the "immanent frame" in which things can be understood as following universal laws without reference to any transcendent reality. This agnosticism allows science to create useful knowledge without having to come to any universal consensus on philosophical and theological issues—it is pragmatic and inductive. This has been a spectacularly successful approach. We would not have the Internet if Newton and Maxwell and Schrödinger had to agree on the fundamental nature and purpose of reality. But when modernity separated the world into "facts," the domain of science, and "values," the domain of religion, it foreclosed the possibility that the two might have something to say to one another.

The consequence of this change has been that creation, a concept connected to goodness and beauty, has been replaced by "nature," a bunch of things without their own purposes, simply there for us to use.[10] In the words of Pope Francis, "Human beings and material objects no longer extend a friendly hand to one another; the relationship has become confrontational."[11]

---

9. It is worth distinguishing between "modern" science, which was more of a nineteenth-century ideal, and "contemporary" science, which is not foundational in the same sense.

10. Historians often point out that Aristotelian science, the kind practiced by Aquinas, included questions of final causality or the end goal of matter, whereas modern science rules these as out of bounds.

11. Pope Francis, *Encyclical Letter Laudato Si' of the Holy Father Francis on Care for Our Common Home* (Vatican City: Vatican Press, 2015), 106.

This change has long concerned me. As an undergraduate physics major, I remember arguments in our classes about ethics and science. Twenty years later, I still remember a quote we encountered from Francis Bacon's describing the ideal experimental method:

> If any skilful Servant of Nature shall bring force to bear on matter, and shall vex it and drive it to extremities as if with the purpose of reducing it to nothing, then will matter . . . finding itself in these straits, turn and transform itself into strange shapes, passing from one change to another till it has gone through the whole circle and finished the period.[12]

I'm sure that Bacon had a more subtle meaning in mind, but to me, it said that the material world has no intrinsic value save what laws it discloses under stress. This is a deep spiritual change that has important consequences for spiritual companionship. If we are encouraged to see the world simply as stuff for human beings to manipulate, it is hard to see that "each creature has its own purpose. None is superfluous. The entire material universe speaks of God's love, his boundless affection for us. Soil, water, mountains: everything is, as it

---

12. Francis Bacon, "Of the Wisdom of the Ancients," in *The Works of Francis Bacon*, ed. Spedding and Ellis (London: Longman, 1857), www.bartleby.com/82/.

were, a caress of God."[13] The world is no longer a sacrament that can connect us with God.

This naked materialism has never been all that attractive. In fact, nature-based spiritualities are on the increase.[14] But this resistance can't erase our culture's deficit in being able to talk about purpose versus talking about utility. When we reach out to serve in a world comprised of things, our imaginations are limited. We tend to focus only on the least common denominator of utilitarianism or begin to see spirituality as a kind of escape capsule from this world. We can no longer generate a St. Francis. For where Francis once preached to the flowers, we can barely muster reaching out to our fellow human beings. There is a deep connection between "concern for nature, justice for the poor, commitment to society, and interior peace."[15] To mature in service, we have to be able to see the goodness in all creation.

Serving Together Even When We Disagree

Reaching out to a diverse world will inevitably lead us into disagreements, especially if we connect our service with our faith. We may find ourselves working with partners that see the world in very different ways, even within our own faith

---

13. Pope Francis, *Laudato Si'*, 84.

14. Deal, "Sanctification Within the Middle Ground."

15. Pope Francis, *Laudato Si'*, 11.

tradition. We may find ourselves reaching out to help those who do not appreciate the spiritual reasons for our actions. And the deeper and more hospitable we try to be in our relations, the more these differences will become apparent.

A fundamental challenge emerges from these differences: How can we work together for the common good in ways that both honor our deepest spiritual convictions and don't force others to abandon theirs? I encounter these situations commonly as I prepare people to become pastoral counselors. People often enter our program with a sense of call that their purpose in life is meant to be lived out through becoming a therapist. Our students come from a wide variety of faith traditions and from many variations within each one. It is not uncommon to have a small group with a Pentecostal African American pastor next to a lesbian Tibetan Buddhist and an African Roman Catholic priest. Because all of these people want to be therapists, they tend to be generous of heart and want to connect with each other. And yet, on matters of human sexuality and other social issues, they simply do not share fundamental convictions. In fact, they may not even be able to understand the internal logic of one another's perspectives. But they have made the commitment to work together and learn from one another in their shared goals of healing others.

From this experience, I have learned that culture wars are not inevitable. However, in a diverse culture, being able to root our service to others in our faith takes practice and maturity. Unfortunately, modernity has tended to approach the relationship between faith and society in two simplistic options: the sectarian option and the secular option. In the sectarian option, there is a shared moral framework that guides the entire community and separates it from working with others, even in shared spaces. In the secular option, convictions rooted in faith are considered out of bounds in public discussions. Neither option does much to promote spiritual development: in the sectarian option, we ignore difference; in the secular option, we ignore faith.

Since a spirituality of service is a full-fledged movement of the spiritual life that takes time and practice to mature, diversity can either promote this maturity or provide it with an insurmountable obstacle. Spiritual companions have a vital role to play in helping their friends navigate difference. Returning again to the image of hospitality, we must help one another make room for the truly Other to come into our lives without being jealous or resentful of their presence.

This becomes especially crucial for those individuals who claim a fluid or hybrid spiritual identity. In order to join others in service, they must be rooted enough in their own spiritual practices and communities to be able to make a contribution. A friendly, least common denominator, "everyone is spiritual" solution will not suffice. Nor will an exclusivity that is primarily concerned with guarding the borders of our tradition. For in the words of the Roman Catholic Thomas Merton,

> I will be a better Catholic, not if I can refute every shade of Protestantism, but if I can affirm the truth in it and still go further.

So, too, with the Muslims, the Hindus, the Buddhists, etc. This does not mean syncretism, indifferentism, the vapid and careless friendliness that accepts everything by thinking of nothing. There is much that one cannot "affirm" and "accept," but first one must say "yes" where one really can. If I affirm myself as a Catholic merely by denying all that is Muslim, Jewish, Protestant, Hindu, Buddhist, etc., in the end I will find that there is not much left for me to affirm as a Catholic: and certainly no breath of the Spirit with which to affirm it.[16]

It is possible for diverse groups to come together in service rooted in their spiritual lives. But it usually takes surprising forms.

Maturing through Hope

Summarizing the discussions above, a spirituality of service runs into four potential obstacles in our current situation: instability, distraction, insensitivity, and disagreement. These overlap in one central way: they discourage looking at the world through any shared, unifying vision for its future.

---

16. Merton, *Conjectures of a Guilty Bystander*, Kindle Location 2438.

Postmodern theorists have declared that our times are defined by the "death of the metanarrative,"[17] that people no longer can believe in big stories meant to explain all of reality, whether these are provided by religion, natural science, or social science.

Capitalism, Communism, Christianity, Freudianism, Medicine, Physics . . . all of these have fallen short of their promise. We are justifiably skeptical, especially given the harm that big theories can do when they are followed uncritically— giving us everything from the Crusades to nuclear weapons. However, this skepticism changes spirituality in a fundamental way, since on the surface, it would seem that faith is just belief in one more metanarrative. If this is the case, why should we embrace it?

The last century has produced several philosophies that suggest that we don't need a grand story after all. For instance, Existentialists have urged us to have the courage to stare the meaninglessness and absurdity of existence in the face and be responsible for creating our own meaning. They argue that this choice will allow us to live authentically in the world in which we find ourselves. Postmodern philosophers have suggested that we learn to enjoy our desires, appreciate discontinuity, and shape ourselves in beautiful and novel ways.

Both of these responses call us to give up trying to grasp for some big theory of everything and embrace our lives as we

---

17. Jean-François Lyotard, *The Postmodern Condition: A Report on Knowledge*, trans. Geoffrey Bennington and Brian Massumi (Minneapolis: University of Minnesota Press, 1984).

find them. But other than liberating others to engage in their own self-creation, these approaches seem to have little to say about a spirituality of service. They are local endeavors, and this makes it challenging to see how to live out our biggest spiritual ideals, such as universal love, justice, and compassion. Some broader sense of purpose still seems necessary if we are to work for a good society. But where can we find this purpose?

In Christian spirituality, any response must include the virtue of hope. Hope links us with purpose. Unfortunately, it takes some effort to define what hope really is—and what it is not. One good place to begin is with Thomas Aquinas's definition: hope is a passion that enables us to pursue "a future good, difficult, but possible to obtain."[18] God's grace makes hope into a virtue by directing our striving toward eternal happiness.

The virtue of hope has several distinct features that help us understand its role in the spiritual life. It is supernatural, filling us with a spirit beyond our power to create—it isn't just something like revolutionary spirit or passion for science. It is a virtue, inclining us to act in a particular way, and therefore something habitual and deeper than a conscious choice. Hope disposes us to work for something that is good, and for Aquinas, goodness is far beyond our human understanding. Finally, it is for a future that is difficult but possible, neither simple nor absurd. While only God can create hope, we can

---

18. Aquinas, ST II-II 17.1.

work to make ourselves open to it and refuse to accept any substitute.

The first thing we must realize is that in Christianity, hope is tied to a story, or even better yet, a drama.[19] The resurrection of Jesus shows us a possible future in which creation reaches its fullest purpose, we are no longer oppressed by evil, and God is fully present to us. This process is beyond our grasp but will, like Jesus, be incarnate in the specifics of history. God does not zap away believers from this vale of tears to some heavenly utopia. Heaven will come out of the history we are already part of.

In this way, hope is indeed linked to a metanarrative, a story that makes sense of all our stories. But unlike the metanarratives of modernity, Christianity is not reducible to abstract first principles that spell out in advance what we should do. It is a supernatural virtue moving us toward a good that we cannot fully know, and the way we pursue it is to open ourselves to go wherever the Spirit leads instead of overestimating or despairing of our own capacities.

And as Aquinas notes, hope does not lead us to anything simple or easy. Too often, people (especially inside the Church) seem to present hope through a set of reassuring platitudes that give us a generic sense that everything will be OK, a way

---

19. Hans Urs von Balthasar's analogy between eschatology and drama provides a rich source for reflection here—there is an interplay of infinite and finite freedom just as between an author and actors. The spirit in which the script is lived out constitutes the drama. See *Theo-Drama: Theological Dramatic Theory*, vol. 2, trans. Graham Harrison (San Francisco: Ignatius Press, 1988).

to ignore our pain. That is delusion, not hope. Hope worthy of the name must take us directly through suffering that most people would rather avoid. In the words of the theologian Jürgen Moltmann,

> Death is real death, and decay is putrefying decay. Guilt remains guilt and suffering remains, even for the believer, a cry to which there is no ready-made answer. . . . It is only in following the Christ who was raised from suffering, from a godforsaken death and from the grave that it gains an open prospect in which there is nothing more to oppress us, a view of the realm of freedom and of joy.[20]

Christianity is the religion that gilds an instrument of execution and puts it at the center of worship. It is not just optimism.

In this way, a Christian spirituality of hope is uncomfortable and countercultural. Our current society has made it easier than ever to avoid others' suffering. We have only intermittent contact with people like us. We are persistently distracted. We clothe suffering in neutral scientific terms that disconnect us from its tragedy. We polarize the world into "us" and "them." With reasonable luck, it will take us a while

---

20. Jürgen Moltmann, "Theology of Hope," in *Jürgen Moltmann: Collected Readings*, ed. Margaret Kohl, Kindle Ed. (Minneapolis, MN: Fortress Press, 2014), Kindle Locations 241–49.

to confront suffering. That is why "hope makes the Christian church a constant disturbance in human society, seeking the realization of righteousness, freedom, and humanity here in the light of the promised future that is to come."[21] Hope makes us engage the world more deeply than we are usually comfortable doing.

Making Room for Hope to Develop

Through restoring a sense of purpose, hope leads us into fearless service of others and counters our culture's tendency toward comfortable niceness. This transformation is at the core of how we mature in service. Therefore, the spirituality of service ultimately revolves around cultivating hope. Two fundamental practices can be helpful in this task: identifying the neighbor and making room. Both invite us to move our egos from the center and see how all creation is interconnected.

Identifying our neighbors comes down to being able to look carefully at the situations in which we find ourselves. Who is there whose voice needs to be heard? What action can be taken to further the reign of God? Who can partner with us in our work? The answer to each of these questions is usually unexpected. We are conditioned to see the world in ways that hide suffering and also hide goodness. We have

---

21. Moltmann, "Theology of Hope," Kindle Locations 281–89.

to open our eyes. In short, we need to practice discernment. There are many classic practices of discernment in Christian spirituality that can foster this awareness. All of them teach us to see the world as God sees it, to notice all the myriad ways in which the kingdom of God is emerging and how we can help foster it, even amid the deepest suffering. Usually, this involves unlearning our habitual ways of seeing the world, which tend to be focused on ourselves and our prejudices.

And when we move beyond our narrow perspectives, we will likely find ourselves called to work with others that we had not anticipated. The diversity of our society can be a gift in this sense, breaking down our old understandings and forcing us to rely on the prompting of the Spirit instead of our egos. Truly new things can develop. For instance, research on interfaith cooperation has identified several emerging practices that help create common ground, such as shared community redevelopment, shared public witness for political action, encounters that acknowledge difference, and focusing on youth.[22] None of these approaches require absolute agreement in matters of morals or doctrine; they require a common problem and a commitment to finding the best in one another. These are essential features of a spirituality of service.

---

22. Pluralism Project, "Promising Practices and Leadership Profiles," accessed October 7, 2015, http://www.pluralism.org/interfaith/practices_and_leaders.

The second fundamental practice is that of making room for the Other, in the words of the Jewish philosopher Martin Buber, not as "it," but as "you."[23] A spirituality of service requires the ability to welcome others into our lives as they are; otherwise we are just gratifying our egos. This is difficult, because to welcome others on their own terms, we must turn over control. This hospitality requires a fundamental practice of self-limitation, kenosis. The theologian Sallie McFague observes that

> kenosis manifests itself in attitudes of curiosity, delight, interest, and openness about the world in which we have mysteriously been "set down" and left to figure out what to do. It is an attitude significantly different from the model of radical individualism, which promotes certainty, absolutism, imperialism, and violence. Kenosis does not know but asks questions, beginning from a stance of appreciation and awe for the wonder of being a wide-awake human being, conscious that we did not create ourselves, and that we must discover who we are. It claims that "another way is possible," from either passive acceptance or violent aggression; it claims that at various levels and by various forms

23. Martin Buber, *I and Thou* (New York: Bloomsbury Academic, 2013).

of self-emptying (limiting the ego's selfish
desires), space is given for others to flourish,
flourishing that not only is good for them but,
in a strange way, is good for oneself as well.[24]

We learn that there is no clear-cut distinction between
our happiness and our neighbor's. We can't be separated. All
creation is inseparable from the rest, since no matter how
closely we look at one aspect, we can still see the traces of
others. These lessons are critical for the large moral problems
of our times such as poverty and climate change.

There are many contemplative practices in Christianity
and other traditions that are intended to combat the selfish
desires of the ego and are essential to this moment of the
spiritual life. Here, we might look again to the Indo-Tibetan
tradition of Mahāyāna Buddhism, specifically the body of
exercises known as mind training (*lojong*), as an example.
Rooted in mindfulness practice, this tradition includes insight
meditations to cultivate *bodhicitta*, universal compassion.
There are visualizations, loving-kindness meditation, and the
practice of "giving and taking" (*tonglen*), in which we breathe
in others' suffering and breathe out compassion toward all.
In ways that are only implicit in Christian traditions, mind
training shows a comprehensive approach toward cultivating

---

24. Sallie McFague, *Blessed Are the Consumers: Climate Change and the Practice of
Restraint* (Minneapolis, MN: Fortress Press, 2013), 144–45.

a spirituality of service that can be a rich guide as we help others develop a spirituality of service.[25]

In the end, spiritual companionship for service is about the slow process of cultivating hope. At one and the same time, we must help one another be audacious enough to hope for God's reign while neither giving up or settling for something too simplistic. Hoping is hard work, and service does not just happen. We must practice discerning our role in the divine drama we find ourselves in. We must continue to work to decenter our egos and make room for encountering others in love. And we must encourage one another to persevere and "trust in the slow work of God . . . believing that [God's] hand is leading you, and accept the anxiety of feeling yourself in suspense and incomplete."[26]

25. Thupten Jinpa, *Essential Mind Training: Tibetan Wisdom for Daily Life* (Boston: Wisdom Publications, 2011).

26. Pierre Teilhard de Chardin, "Prayer of Teilhard de Chardin," *Ignatian Spirituality*, 2010, http://www.ignatianspirituality.com/8078/prayer-of-theilhard-de-chardin.

Questions for Discussion

1 What difference does it make to see service not as merely the outcome of the spiritual life, but a moment in it that needs to be developed?

2 When have you found yourself collaborating on a project with those of very different faith traditions? What has contributed to the success or failure of those projects? Does this suggest some fundamental conditions that need to be in place for collaboration?

3 How would you explain the Christian virtue of hope to someone from a different tradition? What criticisms would you expect? How would you answer them?

For Further Reading

Brueggemann, Walter. *Sabbath as Resistance: Saying No to the Culture of Now.* Louisville KY: Westminster John Knox Press, 2014. A look at how a spirituality of Sabbath counters the oppression of contemporary culture.

Moltmann, Jürgen. *In the End, the Beginning: The Life of Hope.* Minneapolis, MN: Fortress Press, 2004. The most accessible point of entry into Moltmann's extensive theology of hope.

Stabile, Susan J. *Growing in Love and Wisdom: Tibetan Buddhist Sources for Christian Meditation.* New York: Oxford University Press, 2013. An examination of the practice of mind training through comparison and use of Christian imagery.

CONCLUSION

Improvised Spirituality

As I began this book, I said that the attitude I wanted to take toward current cultural trends is one of critical appreciation. While many metaphors might describe this approach, the one that most clearly captures my intent is improvisation. Improvised spirituality not only describes what I hope I have done in looking at these trends, but what readers can continue to do in engaging new trends as spiritual companions.

In his provocative work on Christian ethics, Samuel Wells defines improvisation as "a practice through which actors seek to develop trust in themselves and one another in order that they may conduct unscripted dramas without fear."[1] Using this perspective, Wells demonstrates the ways in which the idea of improvisation can provide novel perspectives on difficult moral problems. Wells's analysis draws especially on the theory of improvisational comedy, including the concepts of the stage, accepting or blocking offers, givens and gifts, overaccepting, and reincorporating.

In improvisational terms, the stage is defined by the web of social relationships and culture in which an encounter occurs. In encountering one another, improvisers pursue interactions that set up their preferred relationship conditions.[2] This work is not done beforehand; it is unscripted and negotiated. Spiritual companionship is interesting in that it explicitly invokes the Spirit as a presence onstage. Therefore, the Spirit is also a participant in the improvisation, transcending our perspectives and sometimes inviting us to move the drama in unexpected directions. The success of this theodrama depends on our willingness to receive this inspiration and use it as the basis for our performance.

In improvisation, the action is carried forward through the ways in which the actors make and receive offers, invitations to respond. For instance, one actor might say to the other, "Welcome to the Tardis. I'm the Doctor." An offer can be met with one of two basic responses: accepting and blocking. In accepting an offer, one makes a response that maintains the

---

1. Samuel Wells, *Improvisation: The Drama of Christian Ethics* (Grand Rapids, MI: Brazos Press, 2004), 11.

2. Ibid.

premise of the offer and takes it forward, perhaps in a creative way: "Hello. I've always heard it is bigger on the inside, but this looks rather unimpressive." Even someone who did not catch the reference to Doctor Who could still accept the offer by playing along: "Hello, Doctor, how did I get here?" This can in turn become an offer to the other party to keep the story going. By contrast, blocking an offer rejects the premise and prevents action from developing by closing possibilities. For instance, one might reject the Tardis by saying, "*Excusez-moi, je ne parle pas anglais.*" In this case, one has even foreclosed the possibility of a discussion in English. Wells suggests that blocking is akin to sinfulness in that it refuses to encounter the Other and seeks to consider reality only within one's own understanding and initiative.

Wells examines the concepts of givens and gifts by noting that we often reduce problems to a zero-sum game, limiting our imaginations. We can see this in the way in which many observers of contemporary spirituality pit the Church against emerging spiritualities. For Wells, there is only one given in Christian theology, God, and in fact, God regularly outsmarts evil through challenging the presumptions that appear to be given. In the same way, a great deal of spiritual companioning can occur through using the imagination as inspired by the traditions of faith to move beyond a simple yes or no answer. Many situations can be received not as the product of harsh givens, but as gifts that call for a response— an opportunity for theological reflection and integration on the fly.

The central improvisatory practice for Wells is overaccepting. Overaccepting is accepting an offer in light of a larger story, accepting without giving up initiative—saying "yes, and . . . ". This response avoids the "sectarian response" of blocking as well as the "responsible realist" response of accepting without reflection.[3] In the case of the Tardis, an overaccepted response might fit the Doctor into a larger, more open story: "Oh good! I've been need of a time machine to talk to Napoleon ever since my dream Friday." We can see overaccepting in the scriptural narrative. For instance, when Joseph's brothers come to him to beg for mercy for selling him into slavery, he replies, "Do not be afraid! Am I in the place of God? Even though you intended to do harm to me, God intended it for good."[4] Through his subsequent generosity, the given of Joseph's justice is turned into a gift that preserves the children of Israel.

Overaccepting also deals with the differing quality of offers. As Wells points out, some offers are "dull," seemingly inconsequential or imperceptive. It is worth adding that some offers are made from positions of power, expecting acquiescence. Through overaccepting, conversations can be deepened and power structures subverted. But the point is not to have the last word; overaccepting is itself an offer.

A final aspect of improvisation that Wells explores is reincorporation. To be coherent, we cannot simply pile one

---

3. Ibid., 23.
4. Gen. 50:19–21.

accepted response onto another. Moving a story forward requires the ability to reincorporate lost or forgotten elements to give meaning and advance toward its eventual conclusion. The future must be contiguous with the past. In the case of spirituality, this past includes the wisdom of its tradition. Therefore, spiritual companions can help others by connecting emerging realities in their lives and the culture to the tradition that helps frame their lives. This last practice of improvisation is ongoing and gradual. Spiritual stories are ongoing, and cannot be tied up in a neat little bow.

In rapidly changing times, improvisation is essential to spiritual companioning. These times are unscripted; even if we wanted to, we could not plan our response ahead of time. Moreover, the usual frames we bring to theological reflection on our times tend toward the extremes of rejection or uncritical acceptance: "people are so shallow these days" or "we have to keep up with the times if we want to be relevant." Improvisation provides a third option, overaccepting. But it also suggests that our dispositions are crucial. Overaccepting can only happen if we are hospitable, curious, and unprejudiced.

In the end, spiritual companioning in these times remains a spiritual discipline. It is only possible if we have cultivated attention to the divine and careful discernment. But above all, it calls for a radical openness, giving ourselves up to God's purposes each moment, saying yes to where the Spirit blows and letting go of our desire for a map.

Questions for Discussion

1 If improvisation is a skill honed through both mentoring and practice, where can spiritual companions look to develop it?

2 Are there situations in spiritual companioning in which a more active response is needed than overaccepting?

3 On what issues do you find yourself tempted to either rejection or uncritical acceptance of cultural changes? How might the practice of improvisation change your response?

For Further Reading

de Caussade, Jean Pierre. *The Sacrament of the Present Moment*. Translated by Kitty Muggeridge. San Francisco: Harper & Row, 1982. De Caussade's masterpiece, which blends together Jesuit, Carmelite, and Salesian spirituality, captures the spirituality of openness that is called for to respond to the current times.

Wells, S. *Improvisation: The Drama of Christian Ethics*. Grand Rapids, MI: Brazos Press, 2004. Wells's explanation and application of improvisation to Christian ethics provides many examples that can be generalized to spiritual companioning.